THE PSYCHIC FEATS OF OLOF JONSSON

BRAD STEIGER

THE PSYCHIC FEATS

Introduction by David Techter

OF OLOF JONSSON

PRENTICE-HALL, INC., Englewood Cliffs, N.J.

The Psychic Feats of Olof Jonsson by Brad Steiger
Introduction by David Techter
Copyright © 1971 by Brad Steiger and Olof Jonsson
ISBN 0-13-732016-7
Library of Congress Catalog Card Number: 75-157724
Printed in the United States of America·*T*
Prentice-Hall International, Inc., London
Prentice-Hall of Australia, Pty. Ltd., Sydney
Prentice-Hall of Canada, Ltd., Toronto
Prentice-Hall of India Private Ltd., New Delhi
Prentice-Hall of Japan, Inc., Tokyo

Third Printing........May, 1972

We would like to thank Miss Amanda Langemo for her valuable services rendered as translator of numerous articles and documents from their original Swedish and Danish.

INTRODUCTION

By now the world knows of the telepathy experiments conducted in connection with Apollo 14. When I saw the initial front-page story in my local newspaper, Edgar Mitchell's "receiver" was identified only as a psychic in the Chicago area. My immediate reaction was "I bet it's Olof Jonsson"—and such it turned out to be. As of this writing, the results of the experiment have not been disclosed, but the mere fact that the ESP test was undertaken is a significant milestone in the progress of psychic research. (It is probably not the first space experiment in ESP; ample evidence exists that Soviet cosmonauts conducted ESP tests while orbiting the earth, though no results were ever published.) Mitchell first heard of Olof in mid-September of 1970. A Florida physician visited Olof at that time to check whether the reports of Olof's ability were accurate. Apparently he was convinced, for soon Mitchell contacted Olof directly and arranged the tests. All parties to the experiment pledged secrecy. Word leaked out, however, and I was delighted to see Olof receive some overdue recognition.

It pleased me to learn that Brad Steiger was writing a book about my good friend Olof Jonsson who richly deserved such ample treatment. I could scarcely think of a better writer to produce it than another friend, Brad Steiger. Since entering the field of psychic literature, Brad has produced a number of notable volumes. All have been carefully researched and well written.

I have known Olof well for nearly a decade now. From the start I was mystified by the enigma of his remarkable talents which remained so obscure to the public eye until recently. Some of the reasons for this emerged as I got to know him over the years, but I still do not completely understand. However, a large part of the explanation is Olof's reluctance to be a "fortune-teller" and build a reputation through readings for clients. In the instances where he has used his psychic ability to aid people in difficulties, he has steadfastly remained shy of publicity and preferred that he receive no credit in public. The telepathy test with Mitchell has now made Olof a minor celebrity but, for all its historic importance, it is more like a climax to the eventful life of a remarkable person. Fortunately for us Brad Steiger has chosen to report in depth the background of this talented psychic.

There are a number of ways in which Olof's abilities are distinctive. I am impressed most of all with the considerable range of his talents. Among the mental phenomena, he is the only sensitive I know who can score so well on conventional ESP cards. Most sensitives dislike card-guessing as impersonal and lacking human involvement. Olof has rather made a specialty of guessing ESP decks, and I have seen him obtain remarkable scores under tightly controlled situations. On one occasion, a deck was shuffled by another witness, then handed to me for safekeeping. Each one present tried to write down the order of the cards. The result expected by chance was five correct out of the twenty-five, and my own correct score was a meager six. Olof apologized for not guessing them all; it seems he had only gotten twenty-four correct instead of a perfect score!

Another instance provided an interesting insight into how Olof's ESP works. We were scheduled to attend a TV filming of psychic phenomena. Olof and his gracious wife kindly offered me a ride to the filming, a northside Chicago shop rather than a conventional studio. As we rode, Olof produced a deck of ESP cards. Following his instructions, I thoroughly shuffled the deck, returned it to its cover, placed the covered deck into an envelope, and deposited the sealed envelope in my shirt pocket, where it remained until Olof dictated his calls as part of the TV film.

As we rode along, Olof would intersperse the conve.sation with remarks like, "Yes, I'm pretty sure of card number thirteen now," and "The bottom card is a circle, absolutely certain." Somehow the deck was being revealed to Olof's mind a single card at a time, and in a completely random order!

While the TV camera was filming, Olof called out his guesses of the cards, still inside the sealed envelope but now lying in the middle of the table around which the guests were sitting. I recorded his calls on a paper that had been pre-numbered with "one" through "twenty-five." He called off the first thirteen cards in order, then jumped on to number twenty-three, called the last three cards, and only then went back to the cards he had skipped. The cards remained on the table during an impromptu "seance" conducted by the sensitives present, and the checkup was the finale of the evening's filming. The results showed that the first thirteen and the final three cards were all correct; the only errors were in the group of cards Olof had skipped over. The impressive scoring made a fitting climax to the film.

Olof has also had considerable success with free-response impressions, of course, as his frequent consultations with police officials testify. I have seen enough instances of this to convince me he could become a famous "reader" if he chose.

I have always regretted that I have not personally witnessed any of Olof's physical phenomena. Mutual friends whose judgment I respect have told me tales of tables levitating and objects flying across the room. I have no reason to doubt their veracity, but have myself not been present on such an occasion Here again, the possession of both mental and physical abilities in the same sensitive is highly unusual.

Olof is unusual, too, in that he is commendably free of the jealousy all too frequent among professional psychics. I have rarely heard Olof say an unkind word about another sensitive, or anyone else for that matter. As a result, he has been able to get along with a variety of sensitives and psychic researchers. He combines a boyish enthusiasm for display of his talents with a genuine modesty.

Yes, Olof Jonsson is both unique and remarkable, and as a human being as well as a sensitive. Let us hope that this biography will bring to Olof (and to its author) the appreciation and recognition so long overdue.

David Techter

CONTENTS

THE PSYCHIC FEATS OF OLOF JONSSON

Chapter One

THE CLAIRVOYANT ENGINEER

On March 7, 1952, Olof Jonsson received a telephone call from Leif Sunde, a journalist, who had witnessed a number of experiments which the psychic had conducted in Varberg and elsewhere. "Olle," Sunde began, "terrible things have been happening in Tjornarp. Thirteen victims have now been claimed by a madman."

"Yes, I have read about them," Jonsson said. "Have the police no leads?"

"Nothing more than what appears to be the *modus operandi*," Sunde replied. "It seems he murders his victim, then sets fire to the house so that no clues can remain. It isn't known whether the crimes are sexual in nature or if . . . ."

"He robs them," Olof interrupted. "He—and it *is* a he—murders, then robs. He does not sexually violate his victims. And he has killed both men and women, is that correct?"

Sunde's voice sounded pleased. "Ah, Olle, you are beginning to pick up some clues. Yes, there have been male victims; however, the madman has chosen more women to suffer the torch than men."

"You have been assigned to do a story on the crimes, haven't you?" Olof asked.

1

"Yes," Sunde acknowledged, "and I wondered if you would consider using your psychic abilities to work with me on the case."

"What have the police to say of your plan?"

"I've already checked it out with the investigating officer in Tjornarp," Sunde said, "and we have his permission to bring you in on the case. Will you do it?"

Olof's fingers tightened around the receiver. He had used his psychic abilities in the laboratory, in the seance room, in the streets of Stockholm, even on a merchant ship in sea waters bobbing with deadly mines, but never before had he employed his unique talents for crime detection. In his late-twenties, he was a man of peace who abhorred violence. Could his psyche pursue a murderer? Could his mind blend, even momentarily, with another mind that gloried in sadistic death?

"Will you come, Olle?" Leif Sunde's voice prodded.

Olof blinked. There were flames leaping up from a corner of his apartment. No, the flames were not really there; he was seeing . . . .

A woman lay bleeding, clutching her abdomen. She was terribly wounded, but not yet dead. The fire began to sear her feet. Her clothing, which had been liberally sprinkled with some highly combustible fluid, burst into flames. She screamed horribly; a painful scream that echoed and re-echoed in Olof's inner ear.

"Yes," Olof told the journalist. "Yes, I will come. I will do what I can to apprehend this murderer."

The flames and the screams were gone now, reabsorbed into whatever mysterious ether had granted them momentary rebirth.

Moments after he had hung up the receiver, Olof dialed his sister, Birgit Persson.

"But, Olof," she protested, after he had told her about his accepting the case, "you know how such things upset you. You have always avoided the sordid and the sensational. You know how such grisly acts will affect your sensitivity! Your psyche is like a sponge. You soak up everything around you. Are you really prepared to absorb all these vibrations of death?"

"In my vision," Olof said, "the woman was crying for help. It is my distinct psychic impression that this psychopath will kill many, many others unless he is stopped very soon."

"But what of the police?" Birgit argued. "Too many authorities welcome a psychic as they would an outbreak of the Black Plague!"

"Leif Sunde says that it is all arranged," the psychic assured his sister. "They are eager for my cooperation."

"Very well then, go!" Birgit said in an exasperated tone. "But don't think for one moment that I am letting you go up there alone."

Olof smiled. He had hoped that Birgit would accompany him, knowing that he would need all the psychic and emotional support available if he were to emerge psychically unscathed from the carnage being wrought in the village of Tjornarp.

Leif Sunde and his photographer, Erling Tollefsen, picked up Olof and his sister at Jonsson's apartment and together they made the forty-mile drive to Tjornarp. Talk of the thirteen murders dominated the conversation, so that by the time they pulled up in front of the police station, Olof felt light-headed and slightly nauseated. If he had not been given such a sincere welcome by the police, he might have changed his mind. Within moments, Olof and his party were being shown the various murder sites by a young officer who had been assigned to assist them in any way possible.

"Are you getting anything here?" Sunde asked, as Jonsson stood quietly amidst the ashes of a victim's home.

"Please, Leif," Birgit said, raising a mittened finger in a gesture of silence. "Just let Olof stand quietly and seek to absorb the vibrations in the atmosphere."

Olof shuddered, opened his coat, suddenly mindless of the cold. "God! It was terrible."

Birgit put an arm around her brother's shoulders. "Did you see it?"

Olof nodded.

"Could you see the murderer?" the officer interrupted. "Could you see his face?"

"No, Officer Hedin," Jonsson said, shaking his head slowly. "But all that blood. And the pain. The terror."

"Olof takes these things into himself," Birgit explained.

Fixing Leif Sunde with a stern eye, she said, "That is why I did not think this experiment to be such a good one. It is too hard on Olle."

Officer Hedin smiled. "It is not that I doubt your brother's ability, but it all seems so incredible. These ashes are cold. The crime has been committed. How can he see it happening?"

"It's no more peculiar than watching him move bottles and read books from another room," Leif Sunde told the policeman. "I was a skeptic, too, until I did an article on him some months ago."

Erling Tollefsen took some photographs of Olof and Officer Hedin standing together beside the charred remains of a victim's home. "Olof," Tollefsen requested, "look mystical!"

But Olof appears dazed on the photographs. His eyes reflect the shock and the horror which he had been reliving.

Later that night, over dinner, Officer Hedin admitted to Olof that he had often read about the demonstrations of the Engineer Jonsson in the Swedish press. "It must be wonderful to have this talent," he reflected, as he poured himself another beer. "To be able to see through walls, to relive the past."

"It has its price," Birgit spoke up. "Olle is really a shy, sensitive man. His talent immediately forces him into the limelight. I think he would rather sit at his drawing board."

"Oh, not really, Birgit," Leif Sunde laughed. "I have seen the excitement in Olof's face when he conducts a successful demonstration of psychic powers, and the skeptics mumble and stammer with their scientific explanations."

Olof set down his glass of white wine. "I am happiest when I can do something worthwhile with my abilities."

"And that is what you are doing now, Olof," Officer Hedin said loudly. "You should have seen the looks on the peoples' faces when it was said that Engineer Jonsson was coming to Tjornarp to help us find the murderer. It was like one of the saints was going to descend on a cloud."

"That's wrong," Olof said. "I am no saint. Everyone has these abilities, if only they knew how to use them."

"Not everyone," Sunde corrected. "Tollefsen is lucky if he can get three out of five pictures to turn out. When I told him to use his psychic powers, the plates came out completely blank!"

"Seriously, though," Officer Hedin's voice boomed above the laughter that followed Sunde's good-natured jibe at his photographer, "you came very highly recommended. Good lord, every professor in Sweden must know your work."

Olof chuckled. "Yes, and there are some who would like to see me burned at the stake!"

"But you could actually see those people being murdered today?" Officer Hedin pressed on.

"Today, it was more like *feeling* them being murdered," Olof clarified. "Perhaps after we visit a few more sites, I will be able to see clearer images."

"You really feel that you will be able to see the murderer himself, eh?" the officer questioned, rubbing his chin thoughtfully.

"If the conditions are right," Olof nodded.

Officer Hedin rose. "It is getting late, and I have a young lady waiting who becomes most impatient," he said, punctuating the reference to his *inamorata* with an exaggerated wink. "Remember to sign your checks. You are the guests of the people of Tjornarp. I'll be by tomorrow morning to drive you. Good night."

"What an earnest and cooperative young officer," Leif Sunde said, as they watched Hedin leave the restaurant. "He stands there so patiently while you soak up the impressions of each site, Olof. He will be of great help to you."

Olof jerked back his head, suddenly startled by a fleeting impression. "Yes," he agreed, snatching at the tail of Sunde's sentence. "Yes, he will be of great assistance."

For the next two days, Officer Hedin drove Olof and his party from place to place, standing by quietly while the psychic went into light trance. On the third day, Officer Hedin handed Olof the charred remains of a rifle. "It is unknown whether or not this may be the murder weapon the killer employed during one of his slayings," he said. "Friends of the deceased are positive that she did not own a rifle, so we have concluded that the murderer may accidentally have left this at the scene."

Birgit sighed audibly. "Why didn't you let Olof see this at once? I told you at the very beginning that if you had any physical clues whatsoever, Olof would be greatly aided by being allowed to handle them. You see, it is an ability called psychometry. By touching the object. . . ."

"Never mind, Birgit," Olof said gently. "Now if I might have a few moments silence. . . ."

The others stepped back, allowing Jonsson a space in which to form his own little psychic universe.

The images began to come almost at once. Brutal, violent images, half-thoughts, frightening glimpses into a mind corroded with perversion.

"W-would you drive us back to the hotel, please?" Olof asked Officer Hedin.

Birgit had noticed that her brother had begun to sway weakly, and she rushed to his side. "Olle, you are so pale. Are you all right?"

"Did you see the murderer?" Leif Sunde asked, moving in closer to the psychic. In spite of the March cold, the journalist had slipped off his gloves and hovered above a note pad with a stub of a pencil. "What kind of a description did you receive?"

Officer Hedin made no move to walk toward the police car. "Don't keep us in suspense, Olof," he coaxed. "Tell us what you saw."

"I saw nothing," Olof said softly. "Please, I would like to rest."

Once they had returned to the hotel, Olof locked himself in his room and stretched out on the bed. But there would be no rest for him until he had solved this mystery. From the very moment that Officer Hedin had handed him that charred rifle, he had seen a strong image of a man. But he had to be absolutely certain. Murder was not an accusation to be handed out as lightly as a parking ticket.

Olof lay quietly for a few moments, achieving calm, acquiring that feeling of harmony that he considers a prerequisite for effective "psi" control. The images began to form. One by one, he would visit the murder sites and see them as they and their ill-fated inhabitants existed before the night of grim visitation.

A woman, tall, blonde, young, sat reading in an easy chair. A knock sounded at her door. Who could it be at this hour? Puzzled surprise, not fear—she knows and trusts her caller. Won't he come in? Is this official business. . . or. . . My God! What is he doing with a rifle?

A redheaded woman is preparing the evening meal. Husband and children have not yet returned from an after-school outing. Oh, no, not the doorbell. What on earth does *he* want here now? Have you come to see Eric? Have you come to. . . .

A large man with his spectacles blown away with half of his face.

A woman barely out of her teens in her first home away from her parents, fighting, not releasing her hold on the rifle. Not letting go until. . .

On and on came the faces of the victims until all thirteen had been cruelly cut down by the murder's rifle. As if he were watching a grisly horror film, Olof's inner eyes were able to perceive even the most minute detail in the montage of violent death.

And in each murder Olof had seen the same cold eyes sighting along the rifle barrel, the same grimly-set features twisting into a grin.

"Who, Olof? Who is the murderer?" Leif Sunde demanded when Olof opened his door to admit the two journalists and his sister.

"You are alone?" Olof wanted to know.

"Yes," Erling Tollefsen answered. "Officer Hedin was called away. Do you want me to call the station house and summon him before you make your statement?"

"Lock the door, please, Erling," Olof requested.

Tollefsen quickly slid the bolt into place, then took a seat on the bed next to Olof's chair. "Okay," the photographer said. "Enough suspense. Who. . . "

"Officer Hedin," Olof told them, "is the murderer."

Birgit gasped. "You are certain?"

Olof nodded. "I saw him pulling the trigger soon after he handed me the rifle. I could say nothing at the time. He would have killed us all; I read it in his thoughts. We were out in the country, away from the village. It would have been easy for him."

"He would have been mad to even have thought such a thing," Sunde objected.

"He *is* mad," Olof told the journalist. "He has killed thirteen villagers in order to steal their money. He has burned their homes in order to hide the clues. Four more lives mean nothing to him."

Sunde let his outstretched arms fall numbly to his sides. "But Officer Hedin has been so cooperative. He has been right by our sides every minute since we arrived."

"Yes, and for good reason," Olof said soberly. "And now we must call his superiors and tell them that their trusted officer is a psychopath."

"But, Olle," Birgit said, shaking her head, "will they believe you? What proof do you have? The authorities asked you to come to Tjornarp to apprehend a murderer. Who expected you to name a policeman?"

"I must try to make them understand and believe me," Olof sighed, "for I know that I am correct."

Leif Sunde volunteered to call the police officials and to request their presence at the hotel. When he returned to Olof's room, he bore a puzzled expression on his face. "They said that they would be pleased to come over to the hotel, but they asked our patience until they could solve another mystery. It seems that Officer Hedin has disappeared."

The next day, Officer Hedin's body was found in the river. He had taken his own life. In his room, the police found a suicide note in which he confessed the murders and expressed his fears that it was only a matter of time before Olof would reveal his guilt.

Nineteen years later, Olof told me that whenever he thought of Officer Hedin's suicide it still filled him with depression. The psychic realizes that the villagers of Tjornarp were spared further attacks, but he only wishes that they might have found some way to have helped the sick man before he destroyed himself.

"Officer Hedin killed because he had a girl friend who made extravagant demands on his poor policeman's salary," Olof told me not long ago. "He took the money from his victims and bought her expensive gifts. But still she demanded more. After a while, killing became easy for him. His conscience became a dead thing within him.

"I fear that this same insensitivity to the value of human life becomes a great risk for those who must fight in a war. I am so sorry for the young men who must kill in Vietnam and other places around the world. It is the hardest to kill the first time, then it can become automatic. Once killing becomes a reflex action, the conscience dies. When I think of all the young men whose consciences we have killed—and then we expect them to come home to the United States as normal citizens—it makes me very sad, and very frightened."

Chapter Two

SWEDEN'S GREATEST PSYCHIC

When I first became interested in writing a book about Olof Jonsson, my first move was to contact Curtis Fuller, publisher of *Fate* magazine. I knew that Curt and Mary were familiar with Olof and his abilities, and I have always admired their editorial position of assuming an objective, no-nonsense approach toward the paranormal. Surely, no two laymen could be more qualified to make an assessment of a psychic than Curt and Mary Fuller. In a letter to me dated December 18, 1968, Curt wrote:

> Last night, at the ISPR [Illinois Society for Psychical Research] Christmas party, Olof called five cards in a row that I selected from a deck after the cards had been shuffled by half a dozen people and while his back was turned. He also successfully named a two-digit number [seventy-seven] that I wrote on the air while his back was turned while other persons watched.
>
> Please understand that the conditions were not laboratory-controlled conditions, but nonetheless, I can see no explanation of how Olof was able to do these things unless he possesses genuine extrasensory ability. Of course, Olof will make mistakes like anyone else. But under casual conditions, the results were absolutely phenomenal.
>
> I personally feel that the one quality that has kept Olof from being recognized as one of the world's great sensitives is that he is sometimes hard to control and brings in certain aspects of showmanship when things get a little dull. Scientists who have worked with Olof tell me that

it is a little difficult to get him to stick to a dull routine, which they require to make their findings impeccable.

Curt concluded by stating his opinion that a biography of Olof Jonsson would be a "worthwhile project" and offering his encouragement and personal assistance.

My second move was to put in a call to David Techter. As book review editor for *Fate*, Dave has offered me some of my most constructive criticism when he felt I needed it, and he has been generous with praise when, in his opinion, he deemed the book worthy of attention. When I called on him to discuss Olof Jonsson, Techter was employed as a vertebrate paleontologist at a major Midwestern natural history museum. Although paleontology might seem somewhere at the other end of the line from psychical research, in January, 1961, David Techter had helped to found the Illinois Society for Psychical Research. He is a member of the American Society for Psychical Research, an associate in the Parapsychological Association, and a member of the Spiritual Frontiers Fellowship.

My interview with Dave began with our taking a few moments to examine a new specimen which he had just received—a fragment of dinosaur bone. This led us to a brief discussion of the true identity of a mammoth sea creature, hastily portrayed by the press as a "thawed" dinosaur, that had been washed ashore on a beach on the Gulf of Mexico.

"But you came to talk of parapsychology, not paleontology, didn't you?" Dave smiled. After we had settled ourselves amidst piles of specimens and stacks of books and magazines on paleontology, reptiles, anthropology, and psychical research, I asked Dave for his opinion of Olof Jonsson's psychic abilities.

"He may be the greatest physical medium in the world today," he answered without hesitation. "Olof Jonsson is certainly unique, as are all the great sensitives. Ted Serios, with his astonishing ability to influence photographic film with his mind, is in a class by himself—as are Joseph DeLouise and Irene Hughes with their string of impressive predictions fulfilled. Each of these, together with Olof Jonsson, deserves to be called remarkable. The really great sensitives are a breed apart, yet each is unique in his or her own way."

Dave went on to describe a number of experiments with Olof

which he had witnessed, and the many difficulties inherent in testing "psi" abilities.

"I once heard a psychologist characterize sensitives as 'field-dependent,' that is, they need an unusual amount of 'feedback' from their audience in terms of attention and approval," Dave said. "Certainly Olof is in his element when he is entertaining a group of strangers with his ESP feats. Yet his more advanced phenomena require extended meditation with, at most, a small circle of close friends."

Techter explained that this apparent paradox had stood in the way of Olof's total recognition by parapsychology. According to his sources, certain parapsychologists had become impatient with Olof because of instances in which, in their opinion, the psychic had mixed in conjurer's tricks with his ESP.

"The tedium of continued testing without an appreciative audience seems to work against Olof's talents," Dave pointed out. "On the other hand, few parapsychologists have the patience to sit quietly in a circle for perhaps several hours in hopes of viewing some of his more spectacular feats.

"The researchers who have spent time with Olof admit to being impressed with his ability, yet frustrated by his inability to demonstrate it under tight experimental conditions. And, of course, those conditions must be met to satisfy the rigid demands of science."

As I thanked Dave and rose to leave, he added an important postscript to our discussion: "I have yet to hear anyone question Olof's sincerity or integrity."

My third source of information about Olof Jonsson's psychic abilities would logically appear to be the parapsychological testing laboratories in the United States which had worked with Olof. I referred first of all to the *Chicago Tribune Magazine* for August 22, 1965, in which Loyola University professor James Hurley quoted Dr. J. B. Rhine in an article on Olof Jonsson ["Man with the X-Ray Mind"]:

> Then in April, 1953, Dr. Joseph B. Rhine of Duke University asked Jonsson to come to the United States. In Rhine's North Carolina laboratory, the psychic could be tested with the most recently developed parapsychological equipment....

Olof accepted the invitation in October, 1953, and Rhine's extensive investigative research upheld and further certified the genuineness of Jonsson's gifts.

As Doctor Rhine said to me [Hurley]: "I find this man to be one of the truest sensitives I have ever tested." When you consider the hundreds of psychics Rhine has examined during the past three decades, the statement amounted to an accolade.

I [Hurley] had been contemplating writing a book on ESP with the assistance of Duke University and, of course, Doctor Rhine. It was thru Rhine that I met Olof Jonsson. The parapsychologist suggested that perhaps Jonsson would prove of eminent value in the execution of my project.

Olof had shown me a number of enthusiastic letters from important parapsychologists here in the United States who had worked with him in ESP testing programs. Shortly after my interview with David Techter, I placed a telephone call to one of the psychical researchers who had tested Jonsson.

Even though the man had written Olof a letter stating how pleased his university's laboratory had been with the psychic's recent visit, I found him at first professionally polite, then coldly noncommittal. Since the publishing explosion had occurred in popular psychic and occult literature, I was told parapsychologists had to be very careful not to appear to endorse the work of any one psychic. Although they had been impressed with Jonsson, it was their consensus that he needed much more testing under increasingly rigid controls. Before our conversation ended, the man strenuously assured me that I should consider him as a spokesmen for the other parapsychologists who had tested Olof.

I could understand the parapsychologist's unwillingness to endorse the claims of a career psychic, but I had been requesting his cooperation in a book about a remarkable sensitive who had earned his living only over an engineer's drawing board. I was disappointed. And even more so, when another psychical researcher informed me that Dr. J. B. Rhine had told him that he was now undecided about Jonsson and considered him difficult to test under strict laboratory conditions.

Enough European medical doctors, psychologists, and academic personnel to sink a college campus have investigated, photographed, tested, and observed the claims and the phenomena of Olof Jonsson in Scandinavia. But scientific one-upmanship seems to demand that one immediately discard and impugn the findings of one's colleagues. On the other hand, it can hardly be denied that in the scientific pecking-order, the beleaguered, always-on-the-defensive parapsychologist has to avoid more pecks than any other researcher.

But certainly, my interviews with Olof indicate that "laboratory conditions" are not always optimum!

Olof Jonsson: A psychical research group in Sweden paid my way over to the United States, then Duke University paid my way from New York to North Carolina. At Duke I was given a stipend to cover my expenses. Dr. Rhine said that they did not have much money and that he wished he could pay more. I had a little money with me at first, but soon it was gone, and I could not cover all my expenses. I stayed there for about a month, then I told them that I must go to Chicago and work as an engineer—an aunt had seen about a job for me. The researchers said: "Not when it is going so fine, you must not go. Why don't you stay another few months?" But I felt that I must go and obtain a job, then return on my vacation time.

"So," I reminded him, "you spent most of your vacation time from 1954 to 1967 with parapsychologists and being tested in their laboratories."

Jonsson: *Ja*, and many parapsychologists, such as Dr. J. G. Pratt, have come back and forth to Chicago to test me whenever they could. Dr. Edward Cox has come to Chicago many times to test me, also. Dr. Cox saw me do many high scores in card guessing. He told me that he would like to publish accounts of these experiments in journals, but Dr. Rhine told him that it was too early. I don't know when he thinks the time will be right.

"Can you tell us anything about your experiments at the laboratories?"

Jonsson: Once, while seated in different rooms, I read seventeen out of twenty-five cards for the experimenters.

Dr. Ian Stevenson is a very nice person. He always appreciates it when I come down there [University of Virginia]. The first time I was down there, he called Dr. Pratt and said some very fine things about me.

Dr. Karlis Osis is also very nice. I remember one experiment we did on a road at night. Two researchers were standing in front of the car with the ESP cards, and Dr. Osis and I were about two hundred feet down the road. I read seventeen out of twenty-five, and Dr. Osis got so excited that he said we must go to Dr. Rhine's home and tell him about the experiment. So we did and Rhine said that was very good and we should go do it again.

Dr. Rhine is a very busy man, and he did not have the opportunity to work with me himself as often as I would have liked. I called twelve cards with him one time, as I recall. I did thirteen one time; fourteen another; and so on, but he was not present when I got twenty-two or twenty-five out of twenty-five. He is very cautious and since he was not always present, he would tell his assistants to file their reports of such high-score card runs.

Chapter Three

THE PARAPSYCHOLOGICAL CARD GAME

Since parapsychologists are under the most strenuous kind of scientific pressure to prove that they are not dealing in "fairy tales," most researchers appear to be enemies, rather than allies of the psychically talented. Psychics complain of the sterile environment of the "psi" testing laboratories; the cold, often unresponsive demeanor of the researchers; and the lack of consideration for the human elements of reward, approval, and understanding to alleviate the dull and monotonous ESP tests. The majority of psychics seem to feel that the parapsychologists should pry themselves away from their laboratories and do more field research so that they might observe both the psychics and paranormal phenomena in their natural habitats.

On the other side of the argument, parapsychologists contend that outside of the limiting conditions of the laboratory, a psychic may be able to employ conscious or unconscious bits of the conjurer's art and elements of showmanship to misdirect a researcher when the true "psi" mechanism is not producing the claimed results.

In Vol. 5, No. 2 of *Tomorrow*, British psychical researcher and ESP tester G. W. Fisk offered a defense of those parapsychologists who "waste time and energy on such a soul-deadening pursuit" as guessing cards. In the article "We

Card Guessers," Fisk answered the question of "why waste precious time with such a child's game?" with this comment:

> I suppose it is because of our innate urge to obtain, first, some statistical proof of the reality of paranormal phenomena, and second, to discover what laws of nature determine the manner of their occurrence. The difficulty with all spontaneous phenomena is that they cannot be controlled, and also, it is well-nigh impossible to find the most crucial weakness of all such experiences—the possibility of chance coincidence.

Dr. Gertrude R. Schmeidler has probably done more research than other parapsychologist on the influence of attitude on ESP scores. Dr. Schmeidler has said:

> The psychological theory which seems most appropriate for ESP data is that ESP functions as other psychological processes do: that defensiveness and over-reserve tend to inhibit it; that negativism and hostility tend to result in meaningful errors; and that good rapport and an open, confident attitude or particularly powerful need states tend to facilitate it. If this theory is sound, ESP successes and failures are potentially useful as an indicator (among many other possible indicators) of morale, and of a person's current level of functioning.*

But even with the scientific justification of acquiring statistical proof and the admitted need for good rapport between psychic and researcher, a great deal of misunderstanding can arise. Parapsychologists often interpret a psychic's cautious manner and his reluctance to submit to laboratory observation as a charlatan's fear of exposure. In spite of Olof Jonsson's generous donation of his time and energies to the researchers at the United States' major ESP testing laboratories, the psychic engineer has not escaped accusations that he may blend elements of trickery into his displays of genuine paranormal ability.

In his review of Prof. Olle Holmberg's *Den Osannolika Verkligheten; Minnen och Intryck av Parapsykologi (The Non-Sensory Reality; Memories and Impressions About Parapsychology)* Dr. W. G. Roll of the Psychical Research Foundation, wrote:

> The parts in the book that are likely to be of the greatest interest to

*Schmeidler, G. R. "The Influence of Attitude on ESP Scores." *International Journal of Neuropsychiatry.* September-October, 1966.

the research worker are the reports of Holmberg's encounters with the Swedish medium, Olof Jonsson, now living in Chicago . . . . From Holmberg's account, it is evident that Jonsson enjoys the role of the showman and may use trickery. On the other hand, Jonsson sometimes produces results which cannot be explained so easily. For instance, on one occasion Dr. Preben Plum (professor of pediatrics at Copenhagen University) placed four playing cards in three opaque envelopes, watched by Holmberg, after which the envelopes were presented to Jonsson. He called three of the cards correctly, the fourth being a partial hit (Jonsson stated that the card was one of the queens; it was the queen of spades). Since Jonsson was in another room when the cards were placed in the envelopes and since the cards were also covered with pieces of cardboard, apparently there was no sensory leakage. . . .

Professor Torben Laurent conducted a number of card tests with Olof Jonsson in his office at the Technical High School in Stockholm, Sweden. Professor Laurent's knowledge of the conjurer's bag of tricks enabled him to keep a close eye on the psychic. The educator later described five tests which he considered ". . .especially difficult to explain as illusory tricks."

As an additional qualification to the experiments, Professor Laurent stated: "Engineer Jonsson had no opportunity to instill hidden technical aids in my office where the experiments were performed. Those in attendance were some of the members of my own family, as well as some of my assistants and their wives. In some instances, Mrs. Eira Hellberg also was present as a passive spectator. Jonsson performed his most interesting experiments with common playing cards and dice, which I, myself, had purchased and placed at his disposal."

Experiment I: Jonsson selected ten cards which one of those in attendance shuffled thoroughly and laid on a chair, face down. Jonsson asked Professor Laurent what the top card was.

"I received a faint notion of the face of the card and gave my answer on the strength of that impression, which proved to be correct," Professor Laurent said. "The same thing was repeated with the other cards, consistently with the correct outcome. Jonsson explained that it was clairvoyance through his intermediation."

Experiment II: Jonsson asked Professor Laurent to shuffle his deck, spread out the cards on his writing pad face down, pick up a card arbitrarily without looking at it or showing it to anyone, lay it in an envelope from his writing desk, seal it, and lay the envelope on the desk. While Professor Laurent was doing this, Jonsson left the room.

"When the job was accomplished, Jonsson was called in, and then he asked to borrow one of my dice. I gave him one, which was uncommonly small, and he tossed it on the envelope. It turned up a five. Then Jonsson said: 'The card is a five of hearts; be so kind as to look.'

"The card proved to be a five of hearts. The card and the dice were photographed, and after the film was developed we could establish the fact that we were not victims of suggestion."

Experiment III: Professor Laurent was given the same instructions as in Experiment II. When Jonsson entered the room, he sat down on a chair a couple of yards from the writing desk and announced that he was determined through clairvoyance to identify the card contained in the envelope.

One of Professor Laurent's assistants got an idea and jokingly said to his wife in a stage whisper: "It's a three of spades."

The man's wife hushed him, saying, "You must not disturb Engineer Jonsson."

After a moment, Jonsson said: "There is a three of spades in the envelope."

"There, you see?" the woman scolded her husband. "Now you have upset Olof!"

When the experimenters opened the envelope, however, they found a three of spades.

Experiment IV: Jonsson wished to conduct a mind reading experiment with Professor Laurent, and he asked the remaining spectators and controllers to leave the room to avoid disturbance.

"We seated ourselves directly opposite each other, one on each side of the table," Professor Laurent wrote in his report. "Olof took the deck of cards, spread them out in front of me, faces toward me, and asked me to think of one of the cards. I asked whether it was necessary that I look at the card, and he replied that it was usually easier to concentrate on a card after one has seen it. I did not bother to look at the card, but thought directly about it.

"Thereupon Olof laid down the deck, and after a couple of seconds he said which card I was thinking of. The test was repeated ten times with successful results. I am acquainted with the theory of reading lip movements and therefore held my lips tight together during the thought-transference procedure."

Experiment V: One evening in the home of one of Professor Laurent's colleagues, Jonsson asked that he be given a thoroughly shuffled deck of cards. When he was provided such a deck, he spread the cards out on a table, face down.

Jonsson asked those assembled to name a card, and with the tips of his fingers, he stroked the backs of the cards until he settled upon one, which he picked up and showed to be the card that the group had chosen at random. Jonsson repeated the test several times with the same successful results.

"The whole thing looked so simple that my colleague asked if he himself might try to perform the experiment," Professor Laurent said. "I asked my colleague to pick up the seven of spades. He picked up half the deck without any success. Afterward, he asked Engineer Jonsson for help.

"Jonsson then said that the fifth card that he would pick up after the one he had already touched would be the seven of spades. My colleague picked up seven cards, and the fifth was the seven of spades."

In presenting a summation of the five experiments presented above, Professor Laurent offered the following observations:

1) None of the experiments were of such nature that Engineer Jonsson could employ possible trained finger dexterity.

2) Jonsson performed his experiments only with cards and dice turned over to him by me.

3) Those present at experiments One through Four had been selected by me alone. . . .

4) On certain occasions, the spectators themselves brought about astounding results.

5) In conference with Dr. John Bjorkhem. . . it was made clear that he thought the experiments were founded on true parapsychological phenomena.

6) In conference with the Danish professor Preben Plum, who through film exposed the medium Rasmussen-Melloni. . . it was made clear that even he believes the experiments are grounded on true parapsychological phenomena.

7) Through correspondence, I have discussed Jonsson's experiments with illusion-groups [professional magicians] in Gothenberg and Stockholm, and no one has been able to explain these as illusionary tricks. Certain members of these groups believe that the experiments are based on true parapsychological phenomena.

"If Jonsson's experiments actually are based on parapsychological phenomena, perhaps an analysis can afford us deeper insight into that mechanism which governs life in common among people. This could have more practical consequences than we imagine at present," Professor Laurent maintains. "Perhaps we shall get a new view on that mass psychosis which hurls great nations into war. Perhaps we shall get a hint of the proper conditions for harmony among people, and this will release a solution to what is indubitably man's greatest and worst problem."

Danish photographer-psychical researcher Sven Turck supervised some twenty sessions with Olof Jonsson at his photographic laboratory in Copenhagen and in some sittings at Lund, Sweden, where Professor Olle Holmberg directed the investigation and Sweden's best known parapsychologist, Dr. John Bjorkhem, was present. On one other occasion, the experiments took place in Dr. Gert Jorgensen's laboratory in Copenhagen.

Turck was careful to record only those of Jonsson's presentations which could not be confused with sleight-of-hand tricks, and he interested himself only in tests wherein no one but he knew the value of the playing card that the sensitive was challenged to reveal. Turck and Dr. Holmberg alternated in being the agent for Jonsson, who was removed to another room and seated under the watchful eyes of an experienced control. According to Turck, Jonsson received the telepathically projected three-digit numbers "in an extraordinary way." The photographer found that Jonsson could call the numbers ". . .just as easily whether I wrote them down or merely thought about them."

Turck writes: "Professor Preben Plum, who also used to take part, willingly demonstrated the method of placing three envelopes one inside the other, and not allowing the stacked envelopes to be let out of sight for even one instant. As a rule, Jonsson provided the number or the card within three minutes. . . .

"I am personally acquainted with artists who publicly perform with telepathy as a speciality. In 1938, I was possibly the first one in this area who structured methods which could be applied at such performances. . . .None of these [mechanical] aids come to mind concerning Olof Jonsson's presentations.

"I do not know whether any biologist dare test the phenomenon of cryptosensitivity within the framework of biology. The phenomenon resembles psychometrics, wherein the medium experiences scenes or receives premonitions of various types [through the handling of objects].

"Olof Jonsson can, in his present state of progress, decidedly rank as a foremost personality in the field of psychical research."

Since I began observing the remarkable clairvoyant and telepathic abilities of Olof Jonsson in the spring of 1969, I have witnessed dozens of incredible acts of psychic wizardry with an ordinary pack of playing cards. I must point out that magic has been a hobby of mine since I was twelve years old and I am quite familiar with the basic repertory of the professional card manipulator. I will also declare that I am capable of duplicating many of the experiments which I have seen Olof perform. There is, of course, one essential difference: as a "magician" I would be controlling the experiment and would have to employ a good many aids—i.e., marked, shaved, or forced decks.

In every instance in which I observed Olof demonstrating his unique powers with playing cards, the deck belonged to someone else and Olof had not touched it at any time prior to the experiment. In nearly every test, Olof did not even come within several feet of it.

Anticipating objections which shall surely be raised, I fully admit that the tests were not conducted under controls as rigid as some investigators might wish. All of these demonstrations were held in an informal fashion in hotel rooms, living rooms, restaurants, and radio and television studios. At the same time, however, Olof was surrounded in each instance by many skeptics, eager to trip him up, as well as by those who recognized his abilities or were content to be entertained. Under the admittedly relaxed circumstances, then, the controls were as tight as one might hope to achieve.

I observed the following card demonstrations of telepathy, clairvoyance, and psychokinesis in numerous sessions over a period of nearly two years. In many instances I participated in the experiment; in other tests, I served as a witness or a controller. For ease in reporting the essence of the demonstrations, I have condensed them and set them down in third person narrative:

■ The participant is asked to draw a card from the outspread deck without turning it over and without looking at it. After a moment's meditation, Olof Jonsson says that he has received an impression of the card and he gives the identity of the card that he is visualizing. When the participant turns over the card, it is seen by all to be the card that Jonsson has named.

■ The participant draws a card from a spread-out deck, keeps it face down, and puts it in his coat pocket without once looking at it. During this step of the experiment, Olof Jonsson is out of the room. While the psychic is still out of the room, he receives an impression of the card that the participant has chosen blindly and at random. He calls the identity of the card from the other room. When the participant removes the card from his pocket, it is revealed to be the card that Jonsson has called.

■ The participant draws a card out of a deck of playing cards, shows it to a witness, replaces it in the pack. Another observer thoroughly shuffles the deck. Olof Jonsson is brought into the room and handed the pack of cards. He concentrates for a few moments, draws a card from the deck. It is declared by all to be the same card which the participant drew in Jonsson's absence.

■ The participant draws a card from the deck, places it in his pocket without looking at it. Another deck, unopened, is handed to Olof Jonsson when he is brought into the room. The psychic spreads the deck on the table, selects a card, calls upon the participant to withdraw the card from his pocket at the same moment that Jonsson turns over the card he has selected. The cards are seen to be the same.

■ Olof Jonsson requests that an observer think of a card and *will* that card to turn up when the deck is cut. When the deck is cut, the card is shown to be, for example, the ten of hearts. The participant protests that he was thinking of the ten of diamonds. Jonsson explains that the ten of diamonds could not have turned up, because he has caused it to disappear from the deck. Since the deck was produced only moments before the experiment and Jonsson has neither touched it nor come within several feet of it, this announcement is met with great skepticism. A search through the deck reveals that the ten of diamonds has, indeed, disappeared.

Jonsson says that he has now received the impression that the participant is sitting upon the missing card. When the participant rises, he discovers the card beneath a loose cushion on the chair. Olof Jonsson has remained on the other side of the table during the experiment and has not approached the participant's chair at any time. In addition, the participant has had no occasion to rise from his seat to allow Jonsson to place the card beneath him.

■ The psychic asks that a deck be throughly shuffled, then handed to him to be held behind his back. He requests that an observer call out the value of a card. As the observer provides the name of a card, Jonsson removes that same card from the deck held behind his back. This test is repeated many times with the same results.

■ The participant is asked to cut a deck of cards which Olof Jonsson has not seen before the experiment. Upon the cutting, the jack of diamonds shows up. This card is placed in an envelope and set under a heavy book. Jonsson asks the observers to decide which card should disappear from the deck. They select the four of spades. The deck is placed on the book, and the participant is asked to place his hands upon it. After a few moments of concentration, the psychic invites the participant to search the deck. The four of spades, which had been present seconds before, has vanished, but it is discovered that the jack of diamonds has reappeared in the deck. When the book is lifted and the envelope opened, the four of spades is seen to have changed places with the jack of diamonds. From the time when the jack of diamonds was placed in the envelope until the envelope was opened to reveal the four of spades, both Olof Jonsson and the sealed card were kept under close surveillance.

■ Olof Jonsson asks one of the observers to select a card at random from the deck. A card is drawn and returned to the deck. The psychic next asks the same observer to thoroughly shuffle the pack. The deck is set on a table and the card selected by the observer is to be the top card. Once again the observer shuffles the pack at great length, but once again when the deck is set on the table, the chosen card has again found its way to the top. According to Jonsson, he has concentrated upon the selected card and willed it always to surface to the top of the deck.

■ The psychic takes the hand of an observer and asks him to think of a card, explaining that the physical contact will aid him in selecting the mentally chosen card from the deck. While the observer concentrates on his card, Olof Jonsson places his free hand on the deck of cards and spreads them face down over a table. When he selects a card, the observer verifies that he had been holding an image of that card in his mind.

■ An observer is asked to shuffle a deck of playing cards thoroughly and to deal four cards face down to Olof Jonsson and four cards to himself. The psychic informs observer that he has influenced the deck in a manner that would make his cards of higher value than the observer's. When the observer's hand is turned over, it is shown to contain three deuces and one trey. Jonsson's hand is four aces.

■ The participant is asked to select a card from a deck and place it in an envelope without looking at it. The envelope is taken by an observer and placed in his coat pocket. After a few moments of meditation, Jonsson announces that he has received an impression of the card and will now send it to the participant. The participant is advised to attempt to write down his own impression on a sheet of paper as Jonsson directs the image to his pen. The participant relaxes, sits quietly for a few moments, slowly begins to sketch a card. When the card is removed from the envelope, it is shown to be the one drawn by the participant.

Chapter Four

A MOST OBLIGING PSYCHIC

Olof Jonsson has been studied, observed, examined, photo-graphed, and investigated by doctors and parapsychologists since he was a very young man. He has sat patiently and guessed cards, levitated vases, or duplicated test passages from randomly selected books for such accomplished psychical researchers as Dr. Paul Bjerre, Sven Turck, Professor Torben Laurent, Professor Sune Stigsjoo, Professor Olle Holmberg, Professor Preben Plum, Berndt Hollsten, Dr. Eric Dingwall, Poul Thorsen, Dr. J. B. Rhine, Dr. J. G. Pratt, Dr. Karlis Osis, David Techter, Dr. Ian Stevenson, and Dr. Edward Cox.

Because of the attention that has been directed toward Olof's "psi" abilities, both in and out of the laboratory, the psychic is constantly being challenged by researchers and skeptics to prove his talents. Such a process can readily be seen to be potentially exhausting were Olof to heed the summons of every doubting physicist who might wish to submit him to a "psychic-busting" ordeal.

On December 27, 1970, the American Association for the Advancement of Science officially recognized parapsychology as a scientific discipline, after the Parapsychological Association had tried for six years to be admitted as an affiliate of the AAAS. Although such recognition is certainly long overdue for parapsychology, it would be naive to assume that all practitioners of the physical sciences are now going to accept the findings and claims of their colleagues in "psi" research without protest. In the eyes of a hard-nosed physicist or biologist, psychical research will seem as amorphous as ever, and the experiments will be considered as nebulous and questionable as they were in the days of Sir A. Conan Doyle and William James.

For nearly fourteen years, Olof Jonsson surrendered his vacation time and a large portion of his energies to various ESP testing and research laboratories in the United States. This book is partly a testimonial to those long, patient hours spent with sincere, dedicated parapsychologists. For those who accept only their own testimony, a book may seem a very poor substitute for having been actually present during one of Olof's experiments. But should this book be examined by someone who has previously held an entrenched position of hostility and doubt toward the psychic world, he might at least consider the possibility that man may be much more than a chance arrangement of biochemical compounds.

Olof Jonsson knows that an individual with his abilities must be ever on the ready. Even a television studio can be instantly converted into a parapsychological testing laboratory.

On October 24, 1970, Sweden's *The Lennart Hyland Show* came to Chicago to film a New Year's Eve television special to be broadcast in Scandinavia. Swedish-Americans Ingrid Bergstrom and Gunnar and Britta Seaborg told me details of the program taping.

"It is one thing to think about an experiment and concentrate on it when you are by yourself with a few witnesses," Mrs. Bergstrom said, "but when you appear on a big television show, you're sitting up on the chair with the spotlight on you and two hundred people watching you. It must make an ESP experiment so much more difficult."

"First they conducted an experiment in card-guessing," Gunnar Seaborg told me. "I think it was eight out of ten Olof got right. Olof said that the last card was a wavy line. Mr. Hyland said that Olof had already named a wavy line. Olof said, 'That's all right. If it is not a wavy line, I will give you one thousand dollars!'

"'Do you realize that one thousand dollars is a lot of money?' Hyland asked him."

Britta Seaborg picked up the narrative thread: "'Oh, yes,' Olof said. 'I know how much money a thousand dollars is.'

"Then Mr. Hyland asked, 'Are you really going to give us a thousand dollars if you are wrong?' Olof says, *ja*, and when Mr. Hyland turns over the card, Olof was right. It was the wavy line!"

Gunnar laughed. "Whenever Olle says he will bet a thousand dollars, I know that he *really* knows he is correct!"

"Then they sat a big box before Olof," Ingrid Bergstrom went on. "Poor Olle is to say what is in the box. Mr. Hyland said, 'Olof, you are supposed to be able to see through walls; you should be able to see through this box.' Well, it was a big box, but that did not mean that the object inside was big. It could be a million different things."

"Only one person on the production crew knew what was in it," Gunnar pointed out.

"The box was covered with Christmas wrappings and they wouldn't let Olof lift it, of course," Britta recalled. "He had to sit before it on the floor. So what would you think of if you knew there could be any one of a million different things in the box, eh? And you've got a bright spotlight on you, so you can't concentrate!"

"Mr Hyland told Olof to sit and think for a few moments," Ingrid said. "I could see that Olle was starting to get a little bit wet there on his forehead. Mr. Hyland said, 'Concentrate, Olof, while we listen to so-and-so sing!'"

"After the song, they came back to Olof sitting before the box," Gunnar reported. "'I am getting the feeling that it is something hard in substance,' Olof said.

"'Well, think about it some more, Olof,' Hyland said, 'while we listen to so-and-so entertain us!'"

Ingrid sighed, grimacing. "Entertainment! So Olof must listen to that too while he is concentrating, and all the audience is sitting there waiting for Olof to say what is in the box.

"So finally Mr. Hyland said, 'Okay, Olof, let us have it. Tell us what is in the box.'

"And Olof said, 'I have a feeling that it is from an animal, and I think it could be an antler from a reindeer.' So the package is opened and up comes a reindeer's horn that they had covered with mink! Olof had been correct."

Olof Jonsson was seven years old when strange things began to happen in his presence.

"I noticed that I could see and experience things which others could not," he remembers. "When I was younger I had believed that others had the same power as I did.

"The first time I realized my peculiar gift of being able to influence objects with a glance or with power of thought was in my parental home in Malmo, Sweden," Olof told me over some after-dinner Blue Nun Liebfraumilch at a Chicago restaurant. Although the psychic generally abstains from alcoholic beverages, he does enjoy a light, white wine on occasion. He and his wife, Betty, had honored me by considering my joining them at dinner as an occasion.

"There stood a bottle on a table in the kitchen," Jonsson went on. "Suddenly I had this overwhelming desire to see that bottle fall to the floor. It did so immediately, and fell without breaking."

And did not such an event fill a seven-year-old boy with fear and wonder?

"No, it seemed to me to be a very natural thing for the bottle to do," Olof said. His soft voice is flavored with a Swedish brogue that has resisted eighteen years of residency in the United States. "Afterward I noticed that all possible kinds of things moved when I only so much as glanced at them."

And the strange talent had begun to grow.

"I used to dream things that later came true. For example, once I saw in a dream how a girl in the neighborhood would break her leg. The incident happened the next day exactly as I had seen it. I often knew what people in my presence were thinking. Sometimes I could answer a question before it was asked.

"At school it was easy for me to learn. For that reason I never needed to make use of the formulas the mathematics teachers gave us to solve problems, as I had discovered how to gain the answers beforehand."

Olof's remarkably blue eyes sparkled with a remembered bit

of childhood mischief. "Once, in order to shine before my classmates, I dreamed of all the answers to a test that we would be given the next day. It was then a simple matter to give the answers to each member in the class. The teacher was quite astonished when he discovered that all the pupils had perfect test papers—even those who were chronically incapable. I don't know if the teacher ever discovered who was responsible for the mathematical miracle, but for my part, it had only been an experiment."

It was difficult to consider the man seated across the table from me as some kind of "stranger in a strange land." Olof Jonsson looks exasperatingly normal. He is of medium height, extremely well-mannered, and has a jovial demeanor. He is the very Scandinavian prototype with light complexion, light-colored hair, and a preoccupation with cleanliness, orderliness, and the preservation of his youth. One knows that Olof Jonsson must be in his fifties, but neither his unwrinkled face nor his conversation betray his precise age.

"When were you born, Olof?" is a question that will bring a prompt reply: "October eighteenth."

One's slightly pressured pursuit: "Yes, and the year?" will provoke a skillful bit of misdirection and hearty laughter.

Nor does Betty, his attractive, full-bodied wife, escape the Scandinavian obsession for establishing one's own fountain of youth through a careful selection of diet and a Spartan regime of positive thinking, regular fasting, and creative resting. "I predict that Betty will lose two ounces a month this year," Olof will tease. Betty, who has just lost twenty pounds on a diet he enforced, laughs: "Oh, you! I'll lose more than that, but I can't look like a teen-ager forever!"

And it is this round-cheeked, hearty personification of the Swedish ideal of the good life, who has been hailed as Master of the Law of Gravity, The Strongman of the Supernatural, and the most powerful medium of telekinetic phenomena who has ever been experimentally controlled.

Olof reminisced about his parents' reaction to his unusual abilities. "My father maintains that one day when I was very small, I was to accompany him to the doctor. When we were halfway there, I said there was no point in our going on, because the doctor was not at home. Father disagreed, saying we had made an appointment, so it was plain that the doctor did expect us. When we got to the doctor's office and rang the bell, we found he had had an emergency call and was not expected home for quite some time."

As far as Olof has ever been able to determine, no dramatic occult powers are to be found in any other members of his family. "My father, however, does have a certain ability 'to feel within him' matters and things—to foresee such incidents as will happen in the future," Olof qualified. His elderly father still lives in Sweden. "And my great-grandmother was clairvoyant in certain situations. She was strongly cognizant of warnings, and she could hear her husband's wagon a long time before the horses drove in through the gate. Great-grandfather was generally quite surprised that she could have the meal in order and served when he came, in spite of the fact that he arrived at times not agreed upon."

Olof Jonsson's great-grandmother was apparently experiencing the peculiarly Scandinavian phenomenon of the *vardogr*. As early as 1917, Wiers Jensen, editor of the *Norwegian Journal of Psychical Research*, wrote a series of articles on the *vardogr*. It appears that the possessor of a *vardogr* unconsciously employs the psychic projection as a type of spiritual forerunner to announce his physical arrival.

"The *vardogr* reports are all alike," wrote Wiers Jensen. "With little variation, the same type of happening occurs: The possessor of a *vardogr* announces his arrival. His steps are heard on the staircase. He is heard to unlock the outside door, kick off his overshoes, put his walking-stick in place, etc. The listening 'percipients'—if they are not so accustomed to the prelude of the *vardogr* that they remain sitting quietly—open the door and find the entry empty. The *vardogr* has, as usual, played a trick on them. Eight or ten minutes later, the whole performance is repeated, but now the reality and the man arrive."

Olof remembers his mother as a woman of a particularly mild and gentle nature. "She was an inquisitive person with a probing mind, eager to seek the meaning of life, and she always had an interest in the things beyond the ordinary—a quality which I inherited.

"Ever since my childhood, my mother and I were always on

the same wavelength. If one can speak of contacts across invisible borders, then they certainly existed between us. When Mother died in the early fifties, I happened to be in California. I needed no message from home. I knew the day and the hour when she left her earthly surroundings."

Ever practical, Olof prepared himself for the engineering profession. After his examination in 1941, he worked at numerous firms until 1946, when he secured a position as a draftsman at the Monarch Motorbike factory in Varberg. It was during his employment there that his mediumistic gifts began to manifest themselves most strongly, and rumors about the mystical Varberg engineer began to spread through Sweden.

"The attention given me was not always of the most desirable kind," Olof recalls a bit ruefully. "It has always been profitable in the eyes of the majority to make fun of things which relate to the paranormal. Fortunately, however, there are also many newspapers and journalists who show a genuinely positive interest in my experiments. All that I ever ask is a truthful presentation."

Olof remembered the time early in his public demonstrations when a newspaper "exposed" him.

"Ahead of time the newspaper had smuggled an uninvited guest into a private seance," Olof said, staring at the rim of his wineglass as if he were seeing the past being recreated. "The experiment was controlled by several witty and mocking men and women, among them two flunkeys of the young journalist who had attended the seance undercover, so to speak.

"During the seance, I repeatedly got a segment of thread to slide off the table and fall to the floor. I stood more than a yard away from the table around which the participants formed a closed circle. The young journalist was the only one in the group who 'saw through' the experiment. He declared, in print, that I had unwound bits of thread from a spool up my sleeve, because no other explanation was 'possible.'"

Olof told me that one becomes more or less immune to "exposures" of this type. "The psychic sensitive who presents serious public demonstrations of his talents must attribute opposition more to lack of knowledge than to ill will. Of course, such an injustice so early in my public testing did demoralize me, but a short time later a newspaper in Hassle-holm gave me an excellent testimonial."

> In Hassleholm, where Professor Axel Ingvar gave the welcoming speech, people were skeptical of Engineer Jonsson's experiments, which were said to be ninety percent successful.
>
> Little by little, when numbers as well as letters that people thought of or wrote down on a slate were directly identified by the engineer, the audience's skepticism began to lessen. When Jonsson readily and easily named which one of seven persons moved a five-card which had been laid out on the table in a northerly direction, when he had no chance at all of seeing it, there was great applause.
>
> The most skeptical in the crowd was a technical teacher who also experimented with "sabotage." But finally it was he who gave the most beautiful testimonial for Jonsson for his undeniable ability and his honest progress into a realm where the science of the West has not yet penetrated. Loud, appreciative applause came to Engineer Jonsson.

Olof has saved the above yellowed newspaper clipping, not out of egotism, but as a reminder of how a preconceived negative attitude may give way later on to positive acceptance.

"One can say that I liberate specific subconscious skills," Olof said. "The psychic power which we human beings have within us is so strong that it cannot be overemphasized," Jonsson stated. "We do not yet know the answer to the mystery of human life. Sooner or later it will be revealed. Until such time, we must forge ahead, investigate, and experiment with the possibilities which serve us. It is necessary to explore our minds to their utmost."

Chapter Five

MORE PSI TRIALS AND TESTS

To thousands of people in his native Sweden, Olof Jonsson is remembered as the "master medium" of the late 1940's. At one point, Jonsson's demonstrations were given such extensive coverage in the Swedish press that many assumed that the Varberg engineer had true supernatural powers. Although Jonsson left his native Scandinavia in 1953, the public demand for up-to-date accounts of his psychic accomplishments has not abated. Numerous Swedish journalists have traveled to the Chicago area in order to interview Olof and conduct fresh tests for the sensitive's many devoted fans and followers in Scandinavia.

On October 24, 1970, the television production crew of *The Lennart Hyland Show* utilized Chicago studios to film a New Year's Eve special which would feature Olof and some of Sweden's brightest actors and entertainers. At the same time, a number of Swedish newspapers and magazines sent reporters to interview Jonsson for special holiday features.

"One of the reporters, Oke Winslow, telephoned me from a hotel to set up an interview with me," Olof smiled. "I had never met him before, so he thought he would try to test me over the telephone and asked me what he looked like. I told him that he had a round face, a beard, and that he had started a bad habit of smoking cigars. He asked me how he was dressed, and I said that he had just come from the shower, so he wasn't dressed at all. He laughed and told me that I was correct. I could see him clearly."

In the November 7, 1965, issue of Sweden's *The Sunday Express*, journalist Lennart Arnstad told of his visit with Olof Jonsson, who at that time lived in a bachelor apartment in Hammond, Indiana.

"There stands a man with round, pink cheeks and clear blue eyes waiting with his new Chevrolet Monza. He wears a blue blazer and well-pressed trousers and his name is Olof Jonsson."

As Olof drove Arnstad through Hammond, he told the journalist that his dream was to quit designing and to open his own research institute. "Now I allow myself to be tested and examined by dozens of scientists," Jonsson said, "but science can only register my experiments, not determine what my abilities are dependent upon."

Olof told his visiting countryman that he had recently participated in three television shows and ten radio programs. "I received thousands of letters after my appearances," Jonsson said, "but I was disappointed at the number that sought to make use of my abilities in lotteries or at the racetrack. At one racetrack I selected a winner in each of the three races I bet on. But this business is not for me. My abilities were not intended to be used in such a manner."

Arnstad pressed the sensitive for an answer to *how* he accomplished his paranormal feats.

"It is difficult to explain," Jonsson told him. "If, for example, I am going to look at the future for a person, I need several hours of concentration. I go into a kind of light trance, see the seeking person's life as a film in my subconscious. It is the same in other tests. I 'see' the cards, for example, in front of me through concentrating on the person who holds them."

Later that evening, in a Chicago restaurant, Olof wrote something on his napkin, folded it, and handed it to Arnstad. "Do not open the napkin," Jonsson told the curious journalist. "On it I have drawn a playing card. Now I will draw another according to your instructions."

Arnstad gave him point by point instructions to draw a five. "Fine," Olof agreed. "Now the suit remains. What do you want?"

"I answered diamonds," Arnstad admitted later, "because that was the only thing I thought of."

"Good," Olof smiled. "Now look at the paper you received from me before we began."

Arnstad unfolded the napkin. Olof had drawn a card with five points with the identification "five of diamonds" written above it.

"This is a café," Arnstad thought to himself. "I am a journalist. I am sitting here with a man whose name is Olof Jonsson and none of this makes sense. . . ."

"Yes," Olof interrupted his mental assessment. "There are seven members in your family at home in Sweden and you have a sister who is eighteen. Two of your brothers and one sister are married."

Arnstad nodded in speechless agreement. Suddenly, two coats jerked off a nearby clothes hanger and fell to the floor.

"Never mind," Olof told him. "It is nothing to be concerned about. Objects often move when I am in the vicinity. I cannot help that. . . ."

The next day, in Olof's bachelor apartment, the psychic bade the journalist shuffle the cards of an ESP deck and hold them behind his back. "Now take out a green circle," was Jonsson's next request.

"I turned the cards over behind my back in order to confuse him," Arnstad later confessed to his readers. "I was a little angry. One must expose this kind of thing. One cannot allow such activity to go on.

"After that I held forth a card—a green circle! My thoughts began to go in circles. How does he do it?"

Jonsson next asked that the journalist select any book at random from the bookshelves in his den. Arnstad's article continues:

"...Now you will read the lines farthest down on whatever page you choose," says Olof. His pink cheeks are glowing with happiness. He is in serious action. "While you are deciding, I'll go into the bathroom. . . ."
    I page through the book, find a phrase at random, a completely

disconnected phrase, split because the page is divided into two columns. It says: "The hub of the Patience Worth (division of columns) tail shortly."

For three minutes I read the phrase over and over again. Take one word at a time until the whole thing almost dances in front of my eyes. Then I hear Olof's orders from the bathroom—to which the door is closed: "Concentrate. . .now relax. . .now. . .read now."

When he comes in, he has a little piece of yellow paper in his hand, perspiration on his brow. On the paper I read, clearly and plainly:

The hub of the Patience Worth—tail shortly.

It seemed there was nothing for me to say. I have not felt anything beyond a deep concentration. Now I feel frightened in the face of the fantastic dimensions of the unreal which is stored up in that little room. Afraid—and impressed.

Much impressed.

In my opinion, one of the most impressive tests of Olof Jonsson's clairvoyance was conducted by the Swedish-American, K. Alex Carlsson, who became acquainted with the psychic through Berndt Hollsten, editor of the newspaper *Saningsmannen's*. On November 5, 1957, Carlsson visited Jonsson's Chicago home in the company of another Swedish-American, Sigge Rydberg. Both men had agreed to put Jonsson's power as an "X-ray visionary" to the test. For that purpose, Carlsson had brought with him a picture, well encased in very heavy wrapping paper.

The three men sat in pleasant conversation around the coffee table, speaking about Sweden and mutual acquaintances for some time. Finally, Carlsson put the package in front of Jonsson and asked him to describe its contents. Rydberg had not seen the picture, so he and Jonsson started on equal ground. Both men could guess that the package held a picture, but whereas Rydberg's powers of observation halted at this point, Jonsson's were just warming up.

"It is an old object," he told the men. "It is, perhaps, several hundred years old. I have a feeling of some beautiful color, something blue—it is a picture. There has been singing in front of it. It is from Europe, probably Spain or Italy. I have an impression of a grayish-white wall and a building which resembles a chapel or a church, possibly a cloister. There are people in the picture. I see a woman's figure—she is holding a child in her arms—she is a Madonna. The child is the Christ child. The Madonna or the boy holds something in his hand which resembles a fruit, and there is a cross. There is yet another person in the picture—Joseph!"

Rydberg looked at Carlsson inquiringly. His friend nodded, most astonished at the accurate description which Jonsson had provided. Carlsson removed the heavy wrapping paper and the Blue Madonna was revealed to Jonsson and Rydberg. In this grouping of the Holy Family, the Madonna's veil is blue. The Christ child stands on her knee and holds in one hand an orb with a cross on it.

"You paid twenty-five dollars!" Olof said, glancing at Carlsson. "You paid twenty-five dollars for the picture."

Carlsson confirmed the fact that he had indeed paid that sum for the painting. He went on to explain that he had first seen the Blue Madonna in the Chicago studio of artist Gerda Ahlm. Miss Ahlm said that she had purchased the painting in miserable condition in an antique shop. Since Miss Ahlm had studied art in Germany and Paris and had worked for the Chicago Art Institute for seventeen years, she felt herself qualified to restore the painting.

According to Carlsson, "Gerda Ahlm surmised that the painting was done in Italy or Spain and was very old. It was painted on wood and unsigned. She regarded herself unable to make any statement about the source of the picture; it would in any case have been only a guess.

"I was able to buy the painting for a very reasonable friendship's price of twenty-five dollars, exactly the amount Olof Jonsson had cited. Who painted the picture and what fate it had undergone before I got it remains presumably an unsolved puzzle. It may have been a part of a triptych or hung on a cloister wall. That people had sung songs in praise of the Madonna before the painting was certainly something Jonsson was right about."

Bess Krigel, Chicago schoolteacher and radio personality at WWCA, Gary, Indiana, declared in a signed statement dated May 31, 1969, that Olof Jonsson had correctly named twenty-five out of twenty-five ESP cards from a deck which had been shuffled by four persons before being sealed in an envelope and enclosed in her purse.

In Sweden's *Home Journal* (July 21, 1959) Stig Arne Kjellen reported an experiment during which a Dr. A. took from his own library shelf a book which he knew that he had not yet had time to read. The book was not opened during the experiment and was held at all times by Dr. A.

"Olof Jonsson was asked if he could possibly read the first line of page 111 and write it down on a sheet of paper," Kjellen writes. "Jonsson shut his eyes. After a minute he took a pen and wrote: 'In allegory there is a real picture.' The book was opened. It was a book by Sigmund Freud and on page 111 the first line read: 'In the hidden allegory the original picture was real. . . .' The page as well as Jonsson's writing was photographed."

In a declaration drawn up and written by the parapsychologist Professor Pr. Plum, strong testimony is given to Olof Jonsson's clairvoyance.

The seventh of March, 1947, we, the undersigned were present at the following experiment performed by Engineer Jonsson. Professor Pr. Plum selected from a deck of cards, which was under his control beforehand, four cards and placed them, without looking at them, into envelopes. Two were put in in such a way that the card was first put into another envelope which was sealed. The two cards, flaps against each other, were put into a single envelope which was sealed. In full sight of everyone, Mr. Jonsson rustled the envelopes around a moment, gave them to onlookers (Professor Plum and Mr. Melloni). Then the light was extinguished and in the course of a few minutes, Mr. Jonsson said: jack of diamonds; four or five of clubs, likely four; eight of spades; a queen—I cannot see which one (added later a black queen). Professor Plum thereupon opened the envelopes in full light. They proved to contain: king of diamonds, four of clubs, eight of spades, and queen of spades.

The undersigned herewith testify that we have seen Engineer Jonsson undertake a long list of experiments which we find impossible to explain without accepting his telepathic and clairvoyant powers. Moreover, he gave proof of his power when, without showing any sign of pain, he performed an act which usually is extremely painful, namely hitting the backside of his hand with full weight against the edge of a wooden table.

Copenhagen, March 7, 1947.

The testimonial reproduced is signed by, among others, two editors, a doctor of medicine, a professor, a state's auditor, a music teacher, a civil engineer, and a university librarian.

Chicago architect Cary Caraway told me of the time that a young woman challenged Olof Jonsson's ability to "see" through walls. They set up an experiment wherein the young lady would retire to her hotel room while Olof would remain in another suite and attempt to follow her movements as if he were some psychical closed-circuit television set. The telephones in the two rooms would relay the progress of Olof's hits and misses. Caraway would man the telephone and relay Olof's impressions from the room in which the psychic sat meditating, and a doctor friend of the young woman would receive these impressions in her room and score them. Without error, according to Caraway, Jonsson correctly described the woman jumping on one foot, holding her hands above her head, staring in the mirror, and so forth.

On August 15, 1970, I asked to test Olof's clairvoyant ability to penetrate a concrete wall. Olof and his wife, Betty, together with my family and I had met for a weekend at the Holiday Inn in Madison, Wisconsin. While the ladies and my children sunned themselves by the pool, Olof and I sat in the Jonssons' room working experiments in psi.

"*Ja,*" Olof nodded in answer to my request. "You go into your room and pick a playing card from a deck. Hold it against the wall face forward and I shall draw it for you on this sheet of paper."

I left the Jonssons' room, walked next door to our own. When I entered our room, I was surprised to see our boys playing cards, since I thought they were at the pool. "Steve," I said to our ten-year-old, "Hand me a card from that discard pile."

Steve reached down and handed me the king of hearts. Could a card be picked more randomly than that?

I held the card to the wall and thumped once to let Olof know that the experiment had begun. After a few seconds, I heard a replying thump. Olof had already received an impression.

When I reentered the Jonssons' room, Olof handed me a sketch of the king of hearts. It was unnecessary for me to tell him that he had been correct. Obviously, judging from the expanse of his smile, he knew that he had drawn my card.

"Now, just how did you see that card?" I asked.

Jonsson: I just count three and there it is in my mind. But sometimes I do not see the card: I get an image.

"You get a picture of people's thoughts?"

Jonsson: Yes, and I feel a sensation when I see a color.

I shuffled a deck of ESP cards. "How do you know which card is going to be the second one down and which the third one down?"

Jonsson: I ask myself in what order this will be. For instance, if you have a deck of cards and you shuffle the deck and I said I want the ace of hearts to be number seventeen from the top, you could shuffle the deck for half an hour, one hour, ten hours, and the ace of hearts will still be number seventeen from the top. When I am one hundred percent sure, I can bet anything.

"How might I learn to do this?"

Jonsson: The best way to learn clairvoyance, the ability to see what is hidden, is to start by trying to determine cards and numbers and different symbols, like those in the Zener ESP deck. Take them behind your back and just touch one card and relax. It is very important to relax. Close your eyes and try to receive an impression. The best way to receive the correct impression is just to relax and take what comes to you without effort.

Let us try something. Brad, take the cards behind your back, cut them anywhere. What shape do you feel now when you are holding it?

"Wavy lines?" I looked and discovered I held a star.

Jonsson: But look at what is at the bottom of the pack, next to the fingers of your left hand.

"Wavy lines! All right, how do I learn to pick up the correct impression?"

Jonsson: By practicing the way I just told you. What symbol would you like me to select from the deck? (I named the circle, and Jonsson proceeded to pick each of the five circles out of the deck.) You should have seen me drive this cardsharp wild when I was in Las Vegas. I always knew what cards he held! And at the tables I could call any card I wanted. Of course, I never win much, just for fun. I do not use my abilities that way.

"All right, now," I said. "Here are the cards. I select one. Before I turn it over, you tell me how you know what it is before either of us have seen it with our physical eyes. I mean, what happens to you mentally? How do you *feel* it?"

Jonsson: It is very hard to describe. I just see it. I feel it first in my mind, then I try to visualize it. When I begin to search for it, to visualize it, it will materialize in my mind.

"What tells you when you are correct?"

Jonsson: The picture is clearer and brighter. Now, remember, make your mind blank. I will help you. I will wait until I feel the right condition, then I will send that card to you.

"Square!" (I turned the card over, and saw that "we" had called it correctly.) "You must have grabbed my brain at just the right instant, because I have always found it nearly impossible to make my mind a blank.

"As a writer, I am always thinking about how I am going to say something on paper."

Jonsson: Let us continue. Just keep shuffling the cards. Take one out anywhere in the deck and as you draw it out, you name it. It will be the card you name.

"This is fantastic!" I laughed, and called several cards correctly. "I'm going to have to work on this. I still feel, though that I'm calling them correctly because you are helping me. Excuse me, Olof, but I've never seen your eyes open as wide as they did just now."

Jonsson: (Laughing) No, I just happened to see something. One of the girls is talking about her leg. Yes, I see now that it is Betty. She is stroking her leg and asking Marilyn whether or not her leg is beginning to sunburn.

"You mean you could see the girls, just like watching a moving picture of them?"

Jonsson: *Ja,* I could see them. I just wanted to know what they were doing and if they were all right.

"You just seemed to look through me, or past me, for a moment there."

Jonsson: Yes, I can sit and talk to somebody while my mind accepts impressions from elsewhere. (Later, when Betty and Marilyn returned to the motel rooms, we learned that Olof had seen true. Betty had been asking Marilyn about the advisibility of applying more suntan lotion at, as near as could be determined, the very moment that Olof's eyes had widened in long-distance clairvoyance.)

"I know that you value your talents highly—so do I—so I do not want you to misconstrue this question: Have you been able to put your clairvoyance to practical use?"

Jonsson: During the Second World War, I put clairvoyance to the most practical use of all—saving my life. I was an officer in the merchant marine, chief engineer. The captain of the ship depended on my clairvoyance many times to get us through the floating mine beds.

"You were kind of a living radar-sonar device."

Jonsson: (Laughing) *Ja*, I was the boss in the machine room, and the captain was the boss on deck. He must have consulted me every day.

I remember the time in October, 1939, when we knew that there were many German mines floating around us. Of course Sweden was neutral during World War II, but a mine does not care about that. A mine will blow anyone to bits without prejudice.

During the night, we were traveling about ten knots. That's not too fast, but it can be dangerously fast when one is crossing a mine belt, and I suddenly received a psychic impression that we were doing just that. No one on deck could see them, but I could feel them. I told the captain about it, and he said, "*Ja*, Olof, maybe it's better if we stop the boat." And we did, so that I might meditate a little.

If we hadn't stopped the ship, I would not be here today. Just when we stopped, we saw a mine bobbing up right in front of us. The crew was all frightened, but I tried to remain calm and peaceful, because I knew that I must achieve the right condition to pilot the ship through the mine belt.

I sat at the top of the deck in a light trance, and I could see everything that was happening and I could see all the mines. I would just point my hand in front of me. Go this way; go that way; to the left, the left, to the right. After half an hour we were out of there and everything was fine. You must agree that in this instance I surely presented a practical application of clairvoyance.

In a personal correspondence to me dated November 22, 1969, Dr. J.J. related another possible practical application of Olof Jonsson's remarkable clairvoyant abilities:

"Through several months of connection with Mr. Jonsson, I am convinced that he possesses ESP abilities which under certain circumstances could have great values. During one experiment, I asked him to read microscopic slides. I presumed that he did not have any knowledge of histology or the pathology of medicine, but he gave a diagnosis of cancer or not-cancer by just looking through the microscope. Telepathy is possible here, but during this experiment I tried to concentrate on a different subject."

In June, 1969, Olof Jonsson returned to his native Sweden for the first time since 1953. Although principal among his reasons for returning to Sweden was to introduce Betty to his aged father on Kalkbrottsgatan in Limhamm, and to his sister, Mrs. B. Persson, Olof quite naturally found time to hold some experiments with Professor Olle Holmberg.

A reporter from the *South Sweden Daily Post Express* was on hand on June 22 to provide record of "An Evening with a Famous Medium":

> Conversation with older parapsychologically interested persons about unexplainable phenomena and performances has often ended with:— Pshaw! That's nothing. You should have seen Varberg's Jonsson. A matchbox that was moved several centimeters by power of thought, heavy tables, yes, sets of furniture, all have been commanded and set into motion by the Jonsson willpower.
>
> The other day this much written-about and much discussed man sat in the well-shaded summer grove of a garden adjoining a house in Djursholm . . . . Jonsson appeared to be distinctly younger than I had thought. Only about fifty years of age. A quiet man, unpretentious, gray-clad, apple-cheeked, hair combed straight back, pale eyes with a mild, ministerial look.
>
> The host, Professor Olle Holmberg. . .puttered about among the assembled, anticipating crowd, many of whom were curious, skeptical, amused. . . .

Even before breakfast one of the American researcher Rhine's ESP card decks had been shuffled and put into an envelope and sealed. . . . It was up to [Jonsson] to say in what order the twenty-five cards lay. . . . It seemed to be a strenuous process which now and then demanded a moment of meditation in privacy on a hillside.

At last all twenty-five guesses were recorded, the seal broken, and cards and record compared. Twenty-two correct out of a possible twenty-five. . .It was a phenomenal result. . . .

Professor Holmberg provided Jonsson with his own signed report of the experiment:

Professor Olle Holmberg's Residence, Stockholm. Statement on two telepathy-clairvoyance experiments with Olof Jonsson. Participants: Olof Jonsson; his wife Betty; my daughter Stina, twenty-one years old; my wife Maj; as well as I, doctor of philosophy, Olle Holmberg.

Experiment I. Stina shuffled a deck of Rhine's cards and put them into their case. It was a matter of determining in what order the cards lay; no one had seen the deck. Clearly under mental influence but without words, Stina named the first three cards, I the fourth, my wife the fifth and sixth. Olof Jonsson named the remaining ones.

The order named by us and by Olof Jonsson was the following:

1. star	13. circle
2. square	14. star
3. cross	15. wavy lines
4. star	16. cross
5. circle	17. circle
6. star	18. star
7. square	19. wavy lines
8. square	20. circle
9. cross	21. wavy lines
10. wavy lines	22. star
11. square	23. circle
12. cross	24. square
	25. wavy lines

All these answers were correct except nine, ten, twenty-two. Therefore, twenty-two right.

Experiment II. I put a card into my pocket without seeing or showing it. After a few hours, Olof Jonsson said the card was the three of spades. Correct.

15/6 1969
Witnessed by O. Holmberg

The famous Varberg's Jonsson had proved to his countrymen that his long sojourn in the United States had in no way blunted his powers of clairvoyance. If anything, perhaps, his mind had become more independent of time and space than ever before.

Chapter Six

PSI AND THE PRIMITIVE MIND

During Olof Jonsson's travels to other lands, he has made it a point to undertake parapsychological experiments with whatever psychically talented people he may encounter. Before immigrating to the United States, Olof visited South America, Canada, China, Japan, and Australia.

"In 1949, I visited the Argentine jungle where I managed to study the Indians and their occult powers," Olof told me. "I happened upon a tribe that had remained completely unaffected by civilization. The Indians were specialists in preparing plants and roots for medicinal use. In addition, I found that their telepathic powers had become particularly well developed."

Once the natives presented Olof with a fire festival in his behalf. "The medicine man walked barefooted across a burning charcoal bed, about six yards long," the psychic remembers."He held a branch in his hand, and while running across the red coals, looked straight upward. After he had walked the coals, he showed me with great pride that he had not suffered the slightest burn."

Olof was aware that some anthropologists and explorers had attempted to explain away the phenomenon of fire-walking by saying that the medicine men have their feet treated with tannic acid. "This, plus their naturally calloused feet from going barefoot, is supposed to render their feet impervious to pain," Jonsson said. "However, I carefully examined the feet of the fire-walker, both before and after his run across the red-hot coals, and I detected nothing unusual."

After the ritual had been performed and other Indians had trod the coals without suffering even the slightest burns, Olof was invited to participate in the ceremony himself.

"The medicine man tried to be helpful by chanting prayers over me," Olof recalled not long ago, "but I knew that I had only to achieve a feeling of harmony, of oneness with the universe and I would feel no pain. Even though I knew that I could, through autosuggestion, shut off the consciousness of feeling in my feet, I decided to rely most strongly on psychic protection achieved by reaching that plateau of calmness and tranquility."

Olof removed his shoes, went into a light trance state, and walked resolutely across the bed of glowing charcoal.

"After that experiment," Olof stated, "I rose in the Indian's estimation. On another occasion, an outstanding medicine man invited me to join him for a stroll inside a pit where a great many poisonous snakes and crocodiles were kept. With a certain degree of hesitation, I followed the medicine man into the cave. The reptiles bothered neither of us. We could walk directly in front of the powerful snouts of the crocodiles without their making a move to grasp us. We could handle the poisonous snakes as if they were household pets. Again, the secret lay in the ability to maintain a state of absolute mental calm."

Olof also found the Australian aborigines utilizing many remarkable mental abilities. "One gets the feeling that the Australian Bushmen are equipped with some sort of thought processes that render them undisturbed by words. They seem to put their faith in intuition."

Once, when in the Australian bush country, Olof heard some natives discussing what the Swedish psychic considered very tragic circumstances. A mother had become separated from her child while visiting the marketplace of a larger village. The baby boy had never been in the village before, and he had only recently learned to walk, but while his mother was occupied in bargaining, he had managed to wander away from her side.

"There goes his mama, now," Olof was told by an English-speaking aborigine.

"Is she looking for her son?" Olof wondered, noting that the woman seemed to be walking away from the village.

No, he was told, the woman had searched for several minutes without success. Now she was returning to her own, smaller village.

"But what of her child?" Olof demanded, shocked at the woman's apparent indifference to her son.

"She will go home and call the child to her. He will come."

Olof opened his mouth to protest the impossibility of making the human voice heard over such a distance. However, it suddenly occurred to him that the woman meant to summon her son through mental telepathy. Curious, he followed the woman at a discreet distance so that he might observe for himself if she could employ a mental radio.

"I followed the woman back to her village and sat some distance apart from her so that I might watch her without disturbing her in any way," Olof recalled. "She would sit very still for a few moments, as if meditating, then go on about her work. After she had repeated this very informal ritual for a few hours, she began to prepare the evening meal. I, too, began to concentrate on the child. I feared for his safety once it became dark. Finally, after about four hours, the little boy came tottering home. He had found his way home over a trail which he had never seen before he traveled it that morning on his mother's back."

Olof Jonsson has stated that he found rich soil for psychical research among the Australian aborigines. "There were natives who could so affect their enemies that the hated ones suddenly and mysteriously found themselves stricken with illness and died. Once I watched a native in the process of hexing an enemy. He simply sketched his enemy's features on the ground and stuck a spear through the picture. The spear apparently served as a physical reinforcement for the thoughts of death and illness which the hexer was psychically transmitting to the victim."

Among the black Queenslanders, Olof met his aboriginal

counterpart: a clairvoyant medicine man who could sketch on the ground the answer to any question a client brought to him.

"The man had absolutely no concept of the world beyond the boundaries of his own hunting grounds," Olof said, "so I decided to test him in a novel way. Before I approached his hut, I drew a coin from my pocket and concealed it in my closed fist. When I challenged him to draw in the sand the thing that I held in my hand, without hesitation he scratched out the image of a five-farthing piece."

During his stay in North Queensland, Olof insisted upon visiting a tribe of Bushmen who lived in a region that was so remote that it was considered taboo even for other aborigines to venture there. The white-skinned medicine man was warned that he would be certain to confront evil spirits along the way.

It has been observed that the national trait of the Swede is stubbornness. If this is true, then Olof Jonsson proved himself typical. His determination to visit the outlying village could not be diverted and, as no one was willing to accompany him, he set out on the trail alone.

"It turned out to be a long journey through a gloomy and barren tract," Olof told me. "When I was perhaps halfway to the remote village, I saw a man coming toward me on the narrow path. Although the trail was so narrow that two persons could not comfortably pass one another, the man continued to tread the path directly in its middle. On and on he came, right at me. He looked as though he were asleep, as if he did not see me at all.

"In order to avoid a collision, I squeezed as closely as I could to the edge of the jungle just as the native passed. And that was the extraordinary thing; even though he would absolutely have had to touch me at least slightly, I felt no contact. It seemed as if he had passed directly through me. . .or I through him. I realized then that I had rubbed the ethereal shoulder of a ghost. Later, when I described the phantom, the aborigines made a great noise and told me that I had confronted one of the evil spirits."

When Olof at last arrived at the remote village, he found the natives frightened of him at first. Then, after a bit, when he made no hostile or aggressive movements, the young men found their courage, and their spears, and began to approach the psychic.

"I could pick up from their thoughts that they intended to kill me," Olof said. "I remained calm and sent the thought to them that I came in peace, that I was a good man whom they should welcome. The primitive mind is most receptive to mental transmissions, and soon the young men began to put away their spears and approach me with gestures of friendship."

After Olof had stayed with the villagers for a few days, he found their tongue to be not unlike that of the Queenslanders, with whom he had been visiting before his trek into the bush country.

"I approached a very old man one day when I noticed that he was sitting by himself talking into the air around him," Olof recalled. "When I asked him to whom he was speaking, he replied that he was talking to a good friend of his who had just died and who had come to bid him farewell.

"'How do you know that your friend is dead?' I inquired. The old man looked at me as if I were a simpleton. 'Because he has just come to tell me that he has died,' the ancient one answered impatiently. 'He has drowned while fishing in a river.'

"After several minutes of conversation, I determined the friend's name, and eventually I was to learn that an individual by that name had drowned while on a fishing expedition to a river of some size a distance away from the village. What the old man had experienced is that which we Westerners would term a 'crisis apparition'—that is, the appearance of a friend or a loved one at the moment of his physical death."

Ronald Rose, an Australian anthropologist and psychologist, began a study of the aborigines shortly after World War II. Impressed with the "psi" abilities of the Bushmen, Rose presented a number of them with a questionnaire that sought to determine the extent of their paranormal attributes. The first two questions were designed to gauge the frequency of the crisis apparition among primitive man.

    (1) Would you know if a relative some distance away died, had an accident, or was seriously ill?

    (2) Has this ever happened to you?

Mr. and Mrs. Rose reported that of all the subjects questioned, ". . .ranging from full-bloods to very light castes, from those who had at one time lived in a tribal state to those who did not even speak the native dialect, only three answered the first question in the negative!"

It was from the second question that the husband-and-wife investigating team were able to receive accounts of crisis apparitions among the aborigines. Almost every native at Woodenbong (New South Wales), where the Roses conducted the bulk of their research, had either had such an experience himself or could cite several friends or relatives who had. As with the phenomenon of the crisis apparition among white people in the Western culture, the existence of an emotional link between the people concerned was the typical, perhaps essential, ingredient. But what, the Roses wondered, made the experience much more common among aborigines than among white people?

> Certainly they do not inhibit such experiences. The natives have a social inheritance of belief in magic—their search for causal explanation has, indeed, barely progessed beyond recourse to mysticism and magic. They are not merely ready to take note of and act on "psychic hunches," but, indeed, seek them. On the other hand, white people do not live in a psychic atmosphere so highly charged. Their outlook is rationalistic, and unless a psychic impulse is of an impelling character, they tend to push it aside as irrational. Frequently, perhaps, it doesn't come to consciousness, or is lost in the welter of sensory experiences impinging on the individual.*

It may be that the mind of a psychic is somehow able to create a suitable mental environment for the functioning of his "psi" abilities, an environment that is less rationalistic, more receptive to intuition and hunches. The great Dutch para-psychologist Dr. W. H. C. Tenhaeff, Director of the Institute of Parapsychology at the University of Utrecht, stated in an article in the September-October 1966 issue of the *International Journal of Neuropsychiatry* that since the beginning of the 1920's, he had been collecting as many facts as possible about

*Ronald Rose. "Crisis Telepathy in Australia." *Tomorrow*, Vol. 5, No. 2, Winter 1957

the personality structure of the paragnost [psychic sensitive]. According to Dr. Tenhaeff, the body of research at Utrecht indicated that the psychic personality stands closer to the primitive man and the child than the more strongly individualized cultural man.

> His or her resemblance to children and primitive men is greater than with the mentally disturbed, though it cannot be denied that among the paragnosts observed by us we also met people whose reactions were psychopathic. Several of the subjects observed and examined by us did not show that unity of thinking, feeling, and willing peculiar to well-integrated. . . people. In my opinion, the cause for this lies more in the field of genetic psychology than in that of psychopathology. In accepting. . . that in telepathy we have to do with "inneren" [discovering within]—this being a phenomenon which is not only closely related to but also subject to similiar laws as that of remembering—then it becomes understandable to us that disintegration [involving here dissociation and domination of imaginative life over observation] is highly characteristic of the subjects examined by us. As archaic man and the child, so the average paragnost is a person in development. . . .

On his visit to the Philippines, Olof was invited to do some experiments for psychologists at the University at Dumaquete. When the academicians had finished with their examination, Olof enjoyed slipping out to the countryside, exploring the back roads, and making contact with the native clairvoyants.

"In contrast to the Australian aborigine, the Filipino in the remote villages was on quite a high cultural level," Jonsson stated. "They are much better informed about the mechanics of their 'psi' abilities, although they may not understand such terms as clairvoyance and telepathy. What is important, however, is that they understand how to use their abilities in a practical way."

Olof said that some of the most sensitive mediums in the villages had established themselves as "telephone stations." If a villager wished a friend in a neighboring village to come over for a chat, he would ask the "telephone medium" to concentrate on that friend on his behalf.

"It would not be long before that friend would come to visit," Olof testified. "This technique also worked if a woman wished to remind her husband to bring home an item from a marketplace. She would simply have the 'telephone medium' contact her husband telepathically and he would never fail to bring home the desired merchandise, be it bolt of cloth or string of fish."

Olof Jonsson strongly believes that psychic abilities manifest themselves in all peoples, all over the world.

"I think it may be inherited more easily in some places than in others," he reflected. "I think, for instance, that it is much more difficult to develop one's psychism in a busy city than it is in a small town or a rural area. In lonely places, where there are fewer distractions, psychic abilities seem to develop much more rapidly. An individual has more time to turn inward, to develop his inner abilities.

"The aborigines, for example, developed their remarkable psychic abilities in past generations because mental telepathy was the only means they had of establishing communication over a distance. They had to turn inward for the solution to their communications problem. It has been the same in Tibet, Africa, South America, and other less technically sophisticated areas.

"And let us not forget," Olof stressed, "that the same thing was true in the Western world before we began to develop the crude signals and sounds that grew into our modern communications system. Now, in most people, telepathy and clairvoyance lie dormant, all but smothered by the telephone receiver and the television set. Oh, they can be summoned whenever the entity is in a crisis situation, but, for the most part, they slumber undeveloped.

"Primitive man has cherished his origin. Civilization has not driven out the need for psyche-to-psyche communication that exists in his daily life. In the case of Western man, unfortunately, he has become *too* civilized. He has forgotten the secrets which make use of the marvelous gifts with which man was equipped from the beginning."

Chapter Seven

A MIND INDEPENDENT OF SPACE AND TIME

"Strictly speaking." Olof Jonsson has declared, "there is no definite boundary between telepathy and clairvoyance—it happens that the phenomena are tangent to each other, which is clear from a number of examples. Clairvoyance, which can literally be translated as 'clear sight,' is independent of time and space. To put it simply, it is a power to sense visually events and things which the ordinary eye cannot see. With clairvoyance, for example, one can see a business transaction being conducted several miles away. One can read a letter or see the values of a card hidden in an envelope or lying in a pack without anyone present having any knowledge of it.

"The ability to see happenings taking place in the future is also an aspect of clairvoyance," Olof went on. "We can attain this state of mind in dreams or through an altered state of consciousness.

"When I am about to try to see something which is not available to my usual senses, I put myself into a half-awake, disconnected state of mind and I try, mentally, to move very slowly to that place I am about to describe. After a while, when I have found the right mental condition, I see what is presented to me."

"In certain instances, when the conditions are right, I can also move back in time and experience happenings that lead into the past. I can walk on streets in strange cities and observe everyday life as it once existed in the past. I can then move myself forward and find myself able to account for the many changing environmental scenes."

One evening in 1953, shortly before Olof Jonsson left Sweden to embark upon a series of tests with the famous American parapsychologist Joseph B. Rhine, he was invited to demonstrate his paranormal prowess for a well-attended meeting of the Swedish Society for Parapsychological Research.

Dr. Paul Bjerre, a well-known medical doctor and psychologist, held up a sealed envelope and told those assembled that he had, with his eyes closed, torn a page at random out of a booklet and enclosed that page in the envelope.

"I performed this task just before I left for this meeting," Dr. Bjerre said. "Since I myself have not laid eyes on what the page contains, telepathy must be ruled out in this experiment. This will be a test of Engineer Jonsson's power of clairvoyance."

Olof took the envelope from Dr. Bjerre and began to concentrate upon its contents.

"Can you give me a phrase or two, perhaps a line from the text?" Dr. Bjerre prompted. "Perhaps you can summarize the general nature of the text on that page?"

"I do not seem to be getting any impression of words," Jonsson replied. He hesitated for several moments. "I. . . I get an impression of a person. . . . "

Dr. Bjerre interrupted: "Do not try to alter the experiment! Do not come up with an impression of me and what I had for dinner. Either quote from the text on that page or give me an impression of the general topic under discussion."

Olof's fingers lightly brushed the envelope, brought it to rest against his forehead. "I get an impression of a person who is almost without clothing. This is not Dr. Bjerre. I cannot receive any text. I believe there is no text on this page."

With undisguised disappointment and apparent irritation, Dr. Bjerre retrieved his envelope, and stepped aside to open it. He stood silent for a long time. At last he burst into laughter and turned to face the audience.

"This is truly fantastic!" he said, holding up a full-page picture of a little boy on a beach, dressed only in an almost non-existent bathing suit. There was no text on the page.

Some journalists from the Swedish weekly newspaper *Songingsmen's* once tested Jonsson's clairvoyance in an experiment held in a home of their choice:

> Jonsson asked us to take a book out of the bookshelf, any book at all. We were to turn down a page in the book, opened at random, with the cover toward us, without looking at the text and pictures. Meanwhile, the experimenter went into another room.
>
> When he came out again, he said: "On pages so and so to the left is a full-page picture of a man. On the opposite side above is the heading 'Harold Hjarne.'"
>
> We opened the book at the turned-down page, which no one had seen ahead of time, and discovered that Jonsson's report agreed exactly.
>
> The next book was one written by Fabian Monsson. Jonsson first named the number of pages correctly. He also volunteered, without having seen the book, to read the sixth line from the top of a page chosen at random. "Write also to the sheriffs in Finland." It was correct.

During an evening of telepathic and clairvoyant experiments at the office of Professor Torben Laurent of the Royal Technical High School, Jonsson agreed to demonstrate some book tests for the journalists and educators there assembled.

"Take out one of the many books on your bookshelves, Professor," Jonsson requested. "In the meanwhile, I shall go into another room. When I come back in, I will tell you which page you have turned to and describe its contents."

When Professor Laurent was certain that Olof was in another room and well out of range of sight and sound, he turned to the bookshelf at his side.

"You must have two hundred books there, Professor," one of the journalists said. "Pick a good one to stump him!"

Professor Laurent smiled. "I'll choose one without any conscious thought at all. I'll just run my fingertips along the covers until. . . I . . . decide. . . to. . . stop! Here! A geography book."

The professor opened the book to a reproduction of an old building—a health spa in Bleking. All present noted the page number and its contents. Someone went to bring Olof Jonsson back into the room. Professor Laurent put the book in a desk drawer.

"I get page eighty-seven," Jonsson said after a moment's concentration.

Everyone agreed that he had given them the correct page number.

"I see an old structure where many people visit," Jonsson went on. "I can smell and taste mineral water. The building seems to be situated in a beautiful park with big trees. And I also get a vision of a white horse that is grazing in a meadow."

The professor and the assembled journalists and teachers agreed that Jonsson had been absolutely correct in his description of the old building at the Bleking spa, but none of them had seen his white horse grazing in the vicinity.

"May I see the book?" Jonsson asked.

Professor Laurent slid open the desk drawer, removed the geography book and handed it to the psychic. Jonsson put his hand on the book, meditated for a moment, then flipped the pages open to the picture of the spa.

"See, Olof?" Professor Laurent smiled. "No horse eating his dinner."

Jonsson returned the smile, turned the page over. There on the reverse side was a picture of a white horse grazing in a meadow.

"'Write a number on a block,' was the next magic order to undertake," wrote one of the journalists who was present that night in Professor Laurent's office.

"I took a block and wrote the figure 159. In the interim, Jonsson had gone off into another room. When he returned, he had a paper in his hand. On it was written 159.

"'Write a number in the air behind my back,' the professor was directed. He drew a large 2.

"'I see two,' said Jonsson.

"Another surprising experiment had to do with a book of stories. One person in the group took the book from the shelf. He opened it to a page, by chance.

"'Read the two top lines silently to yourself,' commanded the engineer. 'Then I shall try to transmit the text to myself.'

"When that was done, he read the two lines word for word."

"In those experiments, when Jonsson gives the page number and the first sentences on the page of a book which he has had no possibility of seeing before, my research has convinced me that it must be clairvoyance and not telepathy that is at work," declared author Poul Thorsen.

Thorsen tells of two other clairvoyant tests which he witnessed in 1953 in Malmo, Sweden, with Olof Jonsson as the medium:

"The editor of the *Sydsvenska Dagbladet* had discussed an experiment with Olof Jonsson. The editor had written his private telephone number on a paper that I had not seen. With the editor at his home awaiting confirmation by telephone, we performed the experiment at my hotel room. Jonsson held the folded paper in his hand for just one instant. Immediately he gave the five-digit number, which no one in the room knew. Therefore, there could be no case of telepathy."

Thorsen describes another experiment wherein Jonsson requested that he write a foreign word on a piece of paper. Thorsen wrote *alegria*, the Spanish word for joy.

"*Alegria* is pronounced with a strong accent on the *i*," Thorsen comments. "Jonsson said quite abruptly: 'Mr. Thorsen has written *alegria!* The interesting thing is that Jonsson accented the word on the *e*. I had been visualizing the word, not its pronunciation, and this seemed to cause Jonsson to place the accent elsewhere. It appears to me that Jonsson actually *saw* which word I held in my mind."

Comments from Olof Jonsson on clairvoyance:

People are generally curious about how I "see" pages of books which I "X-ray." I can explain that I get a visual picture of them in their natural form. Other clairvoyant impressions come as on a film—as when there is a course of action in a motion picture.

Sometimes amusing situations may arise from unexpected events. A Miss P. in Stockholm had long wished to be a part of an experiment. So one day a friend announced that there would be a seance at the home of a family she knew. Miss P. noted the address on a slip of paper.

When she was getting dressed in her best for this visit, she put the paper bearing the address inside her blouse, as this happened to be a place where she habitually kept small, precious documents.

That night when we began the experiments, Miss P. was greatly concerned about appearing too eager. She had never been party to anything of this sort before. She wanted some personal proof of my powers, and so she happened to think of the slip of paper which she had put into her blouse before she left home. She asked suddenly: "Can Engineer Jonsson tell me what I have on me?"

"Yes," I answered, "the lady may now remove the slip of paper she has placed inside her blouse."

It hardly needs to be added that all manner of merriment resulted from my disclosure, and Miss P. was the most amused.

Once, Dr. John Bjorkhem brought a couple of sealed envelopes along to an evening of experiments. On this occasion there were a medical doctor and a journalist among the controllers.

The first envelope gave me an immediate impression of a dead animal, a horse, to be precise. After a few more seconds of concentration, I got the vision of a battle in a German city. Leipzig came into view, and I heard German being spoken. The dead horse that I had previously seen was now alive and bucking —bucking so vigorously, in fact, that it threw off its rider, who seemed to be a very prominent man—a general, maybe even a king. Suddenly I knew that it must be Carl XIV Johan that I was seeing, and I knew that the envelope contained some strands of horsehair that had belonged to his horse.

Dr. Bjorkhem laughed and confirmed the correctness of my clairvoyant picture. "I procured those strands of hair at Skokloster a long time ago," he said, "with the very thought of such an experiment someday. The horse, which stands stuffed at the castle, belonged to Carl XIV Johan and was with the king at Leipzig."

When I held the second envelope, I received an impression of some materials from the ancient past. I got a vision of strange races of people, dark-skinned, but not Africans. I saw a vision of an encampment and people who danced half-naked around the fire, singing loudly. I asked for a map and circled a region in the United States where I said the materials came from, where they had lain in the ground.

"Exactly right," Dr. Bjorkhem admitted. "This envelope contains arrowheads that I found when I dug into the foundation of an old Indian habitation."

"Facts speak strongly for the existence of telepathy and clairvoyance," Dr. Bjorkhem has said. "How these mysterious powers can eventually be joined with our present view of the world is a big question. Recent physics has altered our understanding of space and time and added a better knowledge of the structure of matter. Perhaps, with its new methods of explaining the universe, modern science may also gradually make telepathy and clairvoyance accessible to our minds."

On May 22, 1969, Mrs. R. T. S., who then lived on Division Street in Chicago, volunteered her apartment as an informal laboratory wherein Olof Jonsson could demonstrate his psychic abilities for me and a screenwriter friend, Mike F. I had asked Mike to accompany me because I knew that he was an open-minded skeptic who would be on guard against any trickery, either conscious or unconscious. I had only met Olof three or four times prior to this meeting, and I wanted a "cool head" along to tell me if I had any right to be as impressed as I had been with the psychic. Here is Mike's detailed report of that evening:

"Present, in addition to Jonsson and Mrs. S., were Brad Steiger, Mrs. Jonsson, and a physician introduced as Dr. Andy.

"Mrs. S.'s apartment is a large and roomy one, Jonsson's experiments were conducted in the living room; although in the course of the evening he moved about, entering other rooms from time to time. After about three hours of experimentation, the group moved into Mrs. S.'s dining room and sat around the table in the center of the room. During these experiments, Jonsson either sat at the table with us or wandered into the kitchen or into a small pantry area between the dining room and the kitchen.

"There is a large window in Mrs. S.'s living room, but it is hung with heavy silk draperies which were closed from the time we arrived until we left. There is an ornate mirror hanging over the fireplace in the living room, but it is situated at such a height that it would have been impossible for Jonsson to have 'used' it for spotting cards, numbers and/or other material used in blind experiments. There are two windows in the dining room and the draperies at them were open; however, when in the dining room Jonsson sat with his back to these windows and could not possibly have used them as a reflecting surface. Also, Jonsson does not wear glasses. Jonsson, I think, can be said to have had no recourse to assistance from any of the other members of the group. I refer to the possibility of signals being passed or exchanged. With the exception of a table-turning experiment, all tests were conducted in brightly lighted rooms. There was definitely nothing spooky or hokey about the atmosphere.

"Jonsson's experiments were too numerous and too complex to describe adequately. At one point, I blindly chose a card from the regular deck and placed it, unexamined, in my pocket. No one else saw or handled this card.

"Steiger, at Jonsson's instruction, cut another deck of cards into four stacks, which were left on the floor in view of all of us. Jonsson asked Steiger to select from the four stacks the one that he felt contained the card identical to the one that I had in my pocket. Steiger indicated one stack. Jonsson said that was not the right stack and asked me to select the right one. He said that he would help me make the right choice, even though he stood half way across the room and at no time touched any of the cards in either deck.

"I chose a stack more because I felt impelled to point to it than because I wanted it. Jonsson then spread out the cards in that stack and asked me to pass my fingers over the cards until I felt like touching one of them. This I did. I could feel a strange sensation of energy in my fingers as I pointed to these cards, and it became a kind of warm numbness that intensified each time I passed over the ten of hearts. I finally touched the ten of hearts, which Jonsson then withdrew from the spread. He told me to take the matching card out of my pocket, and that card, too, was a ten of hearts.

"In the runs with the Zener ESP cards, Jonsson called the cards correctly, while I held them behind my back, naming them almost before I could separate them from the pack. I was particularly careful to stand so that the mirror could not reflect the cards I held; and later we repeated the test while I was seated on the couch in such a way that the cards faced the upholstery. Jonsson's ability to identify the cards was equally high.

"Jonsson correctly read the serial numbers of a dollar bill taken from my wallet—while he was absent from the room. He also was able to read my Social Security number in the same way.

"During the evening, Jonsson had three of us shuffle a pack of the ESP cards and then had the cards inserted in their case. The case was then sealed into an envelope which was marked for identification and placed in Steiger's coat pocket. Jonsson had planned to telephone Steiger in a few days after Steiger had returned to his home in Iowa to 'read' the cards over the telephone. Later in the evening, however, Jonsson suggested that if he could go to his home and rest for a short time, he might be able to telephone Steiger and me at our hotel and try a run through the cards in the pack at that time.

"Several hours later, Jonsson did call our hotel and correctly identified the first eighteen cards as Steiger turned them over. He missed the nineteenth card, but correctly identified the twentieth. Flustered at having made a mistake, Jonsson missed the next four cards, but called the final card correctly. . . . The late hour, the extensive tests made during the evening, and the use of the telephone may have served to reduce his accuracy, but having witnessed this test as it took place, I can say that I was, to put it mildly, impressed."

Film star Glenn Ford is among those who have witnessed Olof Jonsson score twenty-five hits out of twenty-five with the Zener ESP deck. Jonsson, along with writer-educator James Hurley and Mrs. Hurley, arrived in Los Angeles on April 27, 1964 to meet with the actor, who, at that time, had expressed great interest in starring in a film biography of Jonsson's psychic career. According to Hurley, before they met Ford that evening, Jonsson vividly described some of the more subtle details of Ford's home to Hal Clifton, the actor's personal secretary.

"Jonsson mentioned the oils portraying bullfighting scenes, the layout of various rooms he had never seen, the red-cushioned stools in front of the bar designed by Ford," Hurley said. "Olof said there was a little doll, dressed in a cape, which stood on the bar. I foolishly dismissed my friend's mental images until that evening when, seated atop one of the red stools, I noticed for the first time the little figure in the cape (actually a poncho). I asked Clifton about the object. He offhandedly replied it was a memento from the crew of Ford's movie, *The Four Horsemen of the Apocalypse.*"

Writing in the *Chicago Tribune Magazine*, Hurley stated that that evening had been spent in relaxed conversation. Those present, in addition to Olof, Mrs. Hurley, and himself, were Clifton, Ford, and the actor's mother.

"As the evening progressed, Olof's faculties became more acute, due to either the refined beauty of the house or the comradeship of strangers who had quickly become friends," Hurley writes. "Ford, an avid souvenir collector, showed Olof a number of objects from films he had made or countries he had visited, and Jonsson psychometrized the articles with great accuracy. The clairvoyant also told of Mrs. Ford's morbid fear of fire. He revealed, with Mrs. Ford's permission, that when she was close to delivering Glenn, a house fire almost took her life. Miraculously, Mrs. Ford escaped unharmed."

Capping that evening's demonstrations, Olof called twenty-five ESP cards out of twenty-five correctly. Jonsson never touched the deck, but remained out of the room until Ford, who controlled the entire experiment, asked him to enter.

The next night Olof and his friends were invited to have dinner with Ford, only to find themselves included in a surprise birthday party for the actor. Perhaps as a kind of birthday present, Olof demonstrated psychokinesis for Ford; when standing by the pool, he moved a glass by mental effort alone.

Morey Amsterdam, an astute businessman as well as a flip and fast comedian, became so excited and enthusiastic after witnessing an Olof Jonsson display of "psi" ability that he, too, began to talk about a possible film treatment of the Swedish sensitive's life story. One night at Amsterdam's suite in Chicago's Palmer House, Morey, his wife, a prominent Chicago industrialist, his wife and daughter, and a young singer starring at the Playboy Club asked Olof to give them a private demonstration of his talents.

Although Jonsson had never met any of those assembled in the suite before that evening, he told them past, present, and future details of their lives. He spoke of the singer's fall from a horse some time before and the injury she had suffered. He gave the industrialist the details of a secret business venture which he had masterminded that very day. He also warned him about an injury which would [and did] take place.

Chapter Eight

TRANSMITTING THOUGHTS
WITHOUT "WITCHES' TRICKS"

Olof Jonsson is well aware that many prejudiced skeptics are prepared to arch their eyebrows when a psychic offers a serious demonstration of telepathy. "Many professional 'mind readers' have tricks that make their stage presentations completely convincing to an uncritical public," Jonsson says. "From time to time, one of these professionals makes a public disclosure of his methods, and that same uncritical public makes the transfer of trickery to the psychic who presents a genuine demonstration.

"In most of these performances," he explained, "the mentalist and his assistant are engaged in uninterrupted communication. Many mentalists employ a code understood only by those involved. There are many different codes, and whenever a professional mind reader comes up with one that is new and workable, he guards it with all the fervor of an inventor keeping his secrets from enemy agents.

"Some methods allow certain letters within the assistant's patter to represent certain numbers or words which can be readily interpreted by the 'medium,'" Olof went on. "Remember, the assistant is usually walking among the audience, and often she is able to use sign-language or even unusual sound effects to transfer the message to the mentalist.

"The most up-to-date stage mentalists make use of a miniature radio set with microphones and receivers secreted in their clothing or hair. This apparatus can permit direct contact between the mentalist and the assistant, thus allowing the medium to become most successful in his impressions."

Olof readily conceded that the best of the "witch-artists" employ a fair amount of psychological knowledge and a skillful use of misdirection and audience manipulation. "Some professional magicians who specialize in card tricks have built up a phenomenally rapid technique of 'card-reading' that can be very convincing," he pointed out. "But you will notice that the card magician always holds the deck in his own hands when he, as a 'mind reader,' declares that he is going to identify a card that someone in the audience has chosen from the pack. He subtly manages to force the selection of the card, and he is able to control the location of the card once it has been returned to the deck."

Jonsson stresses the fact that one gifted with genuine telepathic abilities need not rely on "witches' tricks." In order to achieve effective telepathic transfer, Olof first places himself in a "harmonious state of mind." It is this plateau of mental tranquility, this sense of oneness with the universe, that Olof Jonsson insists must be acquired before one may effectively control any aspect of "psi" phenomena. Spontaneous "psi" may occur at any time without any kind of warning. Such phenomena may be subjectively meaningful to the individual. However, in order to *control* these powers as a psychic of high ability is able to control them, Olof repeats again and again the need for a "harmonious state of mind."

"This state comes about best when one relaxes and frees himself from all irritating conditions and concerns," Olof has remarked. "Become, for a moment, a little island unto yourself. When you feel the conditions are right, try to transmit one letter or a number to someone present. When you achieve a particular point of certainty and sufficient readiness, you can try more difficult things such as the transference of whole statements.

"Personally, I am convinced that this telepathic ability lies latent in everyone and can be brought out to a high degree in certain persons who enter a program of training and development. As with all meaningful goals in life, the development of telepathic ability, or any of the 'psi' talents, demands purposeful practice and belief in oneself," Jonsson stated with emphasis.

"That thought-transmission exists is demonstrated in many ways," he continued. "But the solid causal connection has not yet been clarified. When that happens, we shall find it just as natural to communicate telepathically without words as it is now to speak and to hear. The unknown senses can become everyone's own."

Some years ago in Sweden, a magician by the name of Curtis who specialized in card tricks set out to expose the famous Engineer Jonsson. Curtis maintained that Jonsson was using so simple a gimmick that one would have to hunt long and hard to find another of such masterful simplicity. "And this faker has brought science in to mix with his little card game!" Curtis guffawed in print.

Curtis told the press that he had attended a Jonsson seance and concluded that, although the Varbergs' Engineer had correctly named the value of a playing card from another room, the medium owed his accuracy not to any power of mind but to the fact that *he had peeked through the keyhole.*

A newspaper in the city of Gothenberg reported another seance at which Curtis served as the director and the controller. With the press along to record details of the demonstrations to see that all keyholes were plugged, the frustrated magician found that his thesis of peeking was totally inadequate and he had not really "exposed" Jonsson at all. According to the newspaper account:

> ... In the next card experiment, another in the group was asked to think of a card. He chose the queen of hearts, without being directed by anyone else. Next, Jonsson asked him to mix the deck and to deal it into three piles with just any number of cards in the piles. "Now look to see in which pile the card you chose lies," Jonsson commanded.
>
> The command was obeyed, but the card was not to be found in any of the piles, in spite of repeated searchings.
>
> "Isn't the queen of hearts in any of the piles?" asked the engineer innocently. "No," answered the onlookers.

"Look once more," commanded the engineer, pointing to a pile of five cards.

There lay the queen. All during the experiment, Jonsson had stayed at a safe distance away from the table where the card was. Nor had he needed to rely on any keyhole.

Many other experiments with cards followed, and the effect on those present was unmistakable. Some mind-reading experiments proved to be very special. . . .

The press was also present during an evening of demonstrations in Varberg, when Curtis once again confronted Jonsson.

Olof stood in a corner of the room, holding a small chalkboard in his hands. "Can anyone see this chalkboard?" he asked, shielding it with his body.

Everyone admitted that the board was hidden from view.

"Can anyone see what I am drawing on this chalkboard?" Jonsson queried, as a small piece of chalk in his fingers moved over the board's surface.

"It could be the Mona Lisa for all we know," volunteered a young journalist.

Jonsson smiled, set the chalkboard down so that its drawing surface remained hidden from the eyes of all those assembled in the room. Stepping several feet away from the board, Jonsson announced that he would send an impression of his sketch to Curtis.

Jonsson's maneuver had been at once daring and wise. Everyone knew that Curtis would hardly cooperate in a test of Jonsson's telepathic ability. If anything, he could consciously seek to undermine the experiment.

Curtis replaced his scowl with a more pleasant expression, made a brief show of concentration, then blurted out: "A square!"

Jonsson bade the young journalist pick up the chalkboard, "It's a square," laughed the reporter, as he turned the board for all to witness.

Curtis tried to make light of the experiment, and two journalists began to argue about the role of chance in such a demonstration.

"After all," the skeptical one pointed out, "the square is a basic design. Chances are quite high that Curtis would have named a square or circle or triangle. Jonsson is just a clever observer of human nature and a good guesser."

"But Jonsson could have drawn a flower, a star, a boat," countered the more open-minded journalist. "And why would he choose a man bent on exposing him for the test? Curtis might have deliberately said something like, 'the Eiffel Tower,' 'the Grand Canyon,' 'The Last Supper,' just to show Jonsson up and to prove that his thoughts could not be influenced. Don't you see? Jonsson's power of thought transference made Curtis name a square!"

"Your friend is correct," Jonsson remarked, entering the debate. "I can influence thoughts telepathically."

"Thoughts in the abstract, perhaps," the skeptical journalist snorted. "But you could not influence my thoughts."

"Shall we see?" Jonsson smiled. He asked the journalist to leave the room and to write any letter he wished on the small chalkboard. Olof would seek to influence his thoughts and cause him to write a letter of Jonsson's choice on the board.

"This is a challenge I willingly accept," the journalist said. "Mr. Curtis, I trust that you will control things in this room?"

The magician nodded and waved to the journalist to acknowledge his comradeship.

"Now, what letter shall it be?" Olof asked those nearest him.

"How about a *B*?" someone offered.

"A *B* it is," Jonsson agreed.

A few moments later, the journalist returned, holding up the chalkboard for all to see. On its surface he had drawn the letter B.

He could only sputter when everyone in the room, including Curtis, testified that a randomly chosen letter was the same one that he bore on the chalkboard.

"Well, my esteemed colleague and magician Curtis," the sympathetic journalist asked, "just where will you two skeptics put the keyhole this time?"

During the 1946-47 experiments in the photographic laboratory of Danish psychical researcher Sven Turck, Olof Jonsson conducted dozens of impressive demonstrations of telepathic ability.

"I always admired Mr. Turck," Olof said not long ago. "He worked for several years investigating the paranormal and became regarded as the foremost authority in Denmark on real and pseudo-parapsychological phenomena. He was a capable photographer, and his skill with the cameras was of great advantage in the exposure of sleight-of-hand artists. Turck studied the techniques of illusionists and became quite adept at magic in his own right. He examined the methods used by yogis and whirling dervishes in attaining altered states of consciousness, and he was able to compare these techniques with those used by Western mediums in achieving the trance state. When one entered Turck's laboratory in Copenhagen, he was in for the closest and strictest kind of examination."

One night, after Olof had conducted six experiments under strenuous control, with neither mirrors nor keyholes available to him, Turck turned to one of his colleagues and said: "Record that I with my signature attest to the fact that Engineer Jonsson is an unusual parapsychological phenomenon. He possesses telepathic powers and has a very strong bent toward telekinesis. I predict for him a glorious future in the service of science."

"Professional magicians have often suggested that scientists can easily be led by their noses by clever psychics, who make a practice of exaggerating their paranormal powers," Jonsson said. "But Mr. Turck looked upon the psychic world with the eyes of both the professional illusionist and the scientist. No bogus medium could fool him with the devices of the professional magician and illusionist. And Turck exposed many mediums as either complete charlatans or as being guilty of trickery on a subconscious level."

Olof Jonsson admits that "card tricks" would seem to be the professional sorcerer's special domain, but he controls the cards from an ordinary deck in a manner which no stage magician could ever hope to duplicate.

During one experiment in Turck's Copenhagen laboratory, the Danish investigator placed a deck of cards on the table, face down. Professor Olle Holmberg chose a card from the stack, placed it aside, covered it with his hand, not once turning the card over. No one in the room had been able to see which card had been chosen.

Jonsson picked up a pen and a sheet of paper and without hesitation drew what he felt was on the card. Turck took the paper from Jonsson's hand, held up the sketch of two rows of hearts, three in each row, for everyone to witness. At a nod from Turck, Holmberg lifted his hand and turned over the card. It was the six of hearts.

According to Turck and Professor Holmberg, this experiment was repeated several times with equally good results. It seems that the most significant aspect of such an experiment is that no one in the room had seen the card and could thereby serve as a telepathic agent.

"I'm thinking of a letter," Turck once said to Olof.

"You are thinking of a Z," Olof told him.

And so it went, trial after trial, test after test. But always Olof succeeded in naming the card, the number, the hidden article. It seemed as though not even minor changes in one's line of thought could be hidden from the Swedish sensitive.

"On two occasions during the experiments," Turck said later, "he took my whole chain of reasoning, absorbed it in one sweep—a feat which dispelled all my doubts."

Olof's preliminary comments on telepathic testing and development:

I do not prefer playing cards in my experiments, but I use them, as a rule, at the participant's own wishes. Playing cards are easy to operate and they have the advantage of demonstrating results which may be understood by most people without any especially remarkable manipulations. Several years ago, I decided generally to abandon playing cards and utilize the standard ESP cards—five cards each of five symbols, star, cross, wavy lines, circle, and square.

Other of my regular experiments require that a person name a special color, letter, or symbol. Usually I succeed in calling the right thought immediately. Generally, when I am wrong, it has happened that other persons in the group have "thought" simultaneously about an unlike answer. When this happens, it often turns out that the strongest "thought wave" is the one that comes through to me.

If the conditions are favorable, I seldom have any difficulty reading people's thoughts. Amusing situations can result from my not saying anything when I am concerned about a question of a private nature that proper people freely think, but seldom venture to ask. People who meet me for the first time are usually wondering, in the quiet of their own minds, how old I am, whether I am married, and other personal matters. When I spontaneously give answers to their unspoken questions, they become very confused.

Before I married Betty and I would ask a young lady to dance, I would be terribly amused at the jumble of thoughts that could be bouncing around inside a woman's head. "Certainly," I would say, enjoying her surprise, "I would be happy to take you to dinner. And, yes, I have wanted to see that movie, also. But you'll have to pity my poor wallet. That lobster you wanted is a bit too steep. May I recommend the cuisine at this nice little restaurant I know. Yes, I know that you have never been there, but you have always enjoyed Scandinavian cooking."

Before I left Sweden in 1953, a very good friend of mine from Stockholm asked me to lunch at the dining room at the Kramer Hotel in Malmo. My friend had brought along a feminine acquaintance of his whom I had never met. Before we sat down to lunch, I received the impression that this woman was not entirely convinced of my telepathic talent.

I decided to make her change her mind, and I asked her to think of an idea, anything whatsoever, and write it down on the margin of the newspaper that she carried with her. Neither my friend nor myself could see what she had written. After a moment of meditation, I asked her to take the piece of paper in one hand and to squeeze it hard for a while. After a few seconds of concentration, I received an impression of what was written on the scrap of paper: "I am awfully hungry!"

Completely overwhelmed, the woman admitted: "I am most perplexed. I even wrote the statement in English to make it much more difficult. I surrender unconditionally, but I don't really know if I want to become better acquainted with you. We women like to be able to keep some secrets from the men, you know."

A few weeks prior to this impromptu test, I had been visiting a family in Stockholm. Miss Karin Petersson wrote a statement on a piece of paper at the same time that I, in another part of the house, set down some words on the corner of a newspaper. When we compared our papers, literally the same statement appeared on both. On another slip of paper, I had written what her comment would be when she discovered the results of the experiment. In front of the witnesses for the test, I handed her a folded piece of paper which contained a pre-echo of her words: "Is this possible?"

"Can you get into an animal's subconscious the way you get into a human's?" I asked Olof.

Jonsson: Yes, I have done this many times. In one test I concentrated on a cat to do many different things, like go from that corner to this corner, now lick your left front paw, now scratch your ear—things like that. Most cats or dogs respond to telepathic direction, but some do not.

"Can you see what an animal is thinking in the same manner that you can see what an old man on the commuter train is thinking?"

Jonsson: I can get what they feel and what they want, and so on. If the animal has pain, I will know this, even if no one else knows it. If the animal feels low, depressed; if there is a heavy atmosphere around the animal, then I will feel that, too.

"You pick up images and impressions in a human's mind. Do you ever receive images from an animal's brain?"

Jonsson: Sometimes, but is is very difficult to do, because an animal does not think as we do.

"How do they think?"

Jonsson: Well, I am able to see that an animal has imagination in a manner similar to ours. They don't think too much, though, and they seldom plan too far ahead. Mainly, they act spontaneously, according to nature.

"Do you feel that they have souls?"

Jonsson: Oh, yes. Everything in nature has a soul in one way or another. The material part of plants and animals die here, just as we do. You are like a vegetable, but with a bit more understanding. I believe that a flower has intelligence. I believe that every living thing has intelligence of higher or lower degree.

Stig Arne Kjellen arranged numerous unique tests of Olof Jonsson's telepathic ability before the Swedish sensitive emigrated to the United States. "I was able to arrange these experiments completely according to my own wishes," Kjellen said. "Olof generously cooperated in literally thousands of demonstrations."

On one occasion Olof was locked in a room together with Dr. Henrik Carlstrom, who was to serve as control. Kjellen placed himself in an adjoining room and drew out a card from a sealed deck. "Through the locked door and with Dr. Carlstrom insuring that Olof stood with his back to the door, I commanded Jonsson to think of the card that I had just chosen. He immediately named the correct card. We repeated the experiment thirty-six times. Jonsson correctly named the card a total of thirty times."

For another test, Olof was locked in a room with two controllers while Kjellen stayed in an adjoining room. Kjellen wrote three digits on a sheet of paper, which he immediately crumpled in his fist. Jonsson sat in a corner of the next room with his back to the locked door. His task was to write down the three digits on a drawing board held by the controllers. In a few moments, the controllers entered the room in which Kjellen sat alone with the crumpled paper wadded in his fist and revealed the number which Jonsson had recorded on the drawing board: 389. Kjellen unwadded the sheet on which he had written the test number; it was 389.

"This experiment was repeated twelve times in a row," Kjellen reported. "Of the twelve number combinations, each consisting of three digits, eight were completely right, two off by one digit, and two more entirely wrong. Both Jonsson's and my sheets of paper were photographed to preclude all possibility of suggestion."

Professor Preben Plum served as the controller, locked in a room with Jonsson, when Dr. Henrik Carlstrom in a separate room wrote in Danish: "I allow myself to quote. . . . "

"After sixty seconds, Professor Plum came out of the room with Jonsson's version, written in Swedish with the witty variation: 'I, too, allow myself to quote,'" Kjellen records.

For the next experiment that session, Professor Plum and Dr. Carlstrom changed roles, with Carlstrom serving as Olof's controller and Plum writing the message for telepathic transfer. "Do you remember Stockholm's bloodbath?" Professor Plum wrote.

Olof's version: "Do you remember Stockholm?"

Such demonstrations were repeated six times in a row with equally successful outcomes.

"The most interesting of the telepathic experiments Olof Jonsson and I did before his leaving for America began quite spontaneously," Kjellen has said. "I got the idea for these tests, because on several occasions, completely unexpectedly and suddenly, I met Olof in a crowd in Stockholm and he jokingly commented: 'I sensed that you were here somewhere.'"

After a few such "accidental" meetings, Olof agreed to a test of his ability to become a telepathic bloodhound. The terms for the test were dictated solely by Stig Arne Kjellen:

"At exactly eight o'clock the following evening, Olof should concentrate and try with telepathy [or whatever power he could muster] to determine where in Stockholm I might be. As soon as he 'located' me, he was to go to that spot."

Olof went to the apartment of a friend of Kjellen's at seven P.M. The friend was to be Jonsson's control and insure his staying off the streets of Stockholm until after eight.

"At precisely eight o'clock," Kjellen said, "I placed myself in the vicinity of the Dramatic Theater. A few minutes after eight, Jonsson asked if he might leave my friend's apartment. My friend consented and allowed him to go to look for me. After a half hour, Jonsson came walking right to the place where I had hidden. Though I was not visible from the street, I wished to guard against any element of chance having entered into our experiment. We agreed to repeat the test on the following evening."

At nine the next evening, Kjellen placed himself on an out-of-the way park bench in Stockholm's *Gamla Stan*, the Old Quarter. The test arrangements were identical to those of the preceding evening. Jonsson was to be restrained in the friend's apartment, under control, until after nine.

"It was just a little past ten o'clock when Olof arrived with his usual quiet laughter, hardly surprised at all," Kjellen writes.

Kjellen conducted a total of eight such tests of Olof Jonsson's telepathic ability to seek and to find a person who might be hiding anywhere in the streets and shops of Stockholm, a city at that time of approximately 700,000 persons. Olof tracked his quarry successfully five times out of eight. Kjellen feels that it would be impossible for chance to permit coincidental meetings five times out of eight in a city of that size.

In summation of their telepathic tests of hide-and-go-seek, Kjellen wrote:

"The tests, I am afraid, were not carried out with all desired control, and therefore no 'scientific quality' can be allotted to them. I am, however, convinced that similar experiments, undertaken on a broader scale and with control of witnesses and excluding all 'cheating' and possibilities of error, would have succeeded to the extent which would have proved scientifically that accomplishments of this kind are possible."

On May 8, 1970, Chicago architect Cary Caraway witnessed a sketch-transmission experiment. Olof Jonsson served as the agent—the broadcaster—and Mrs. Marge Hospodar served as the receptor. The test was conducted at the Illini Union Building on the University of Illinois Medical Center campus. Those present, in addition to Caraway, Jonsson, and Mrs. Hospodar, were Betty Jonsson, Luke Salmon, Emil Hospodar, and Mrs. Caraway. According to Caraway's written report:

"We were all gathered around a conference table—the women at one end, chatting away, and the men at the other. Olof made a sketch of a flower without any of those present being able to see it and passed it, upside down, across the table to Emil Hospodar and myself. Then he turned to Marge Hospodar, who was sitting across the table and approximately six feet down from him and said, "I have made a sketch. See if you can duplicate it."

"Marge hesitated.

"Olof encouraged her. 'Go ahead. Draw the first thing that comes into your mind.'

"Marge replied: 'But I was thinking of something before you asked me, and I can't think of anything else.'

"'All right, go ahead and draw that,' Olof said. [Olof has told me that he usually starts transmitting before he makes the other person aware of the nature of the experiment.]

"The enclosed sketches of flowers by Marge and Olof constitute the result. To me, this is an indisputable case of mentally sending and receiving an image by other than normal means."

Dr. Charles T. Tart states that the notion of telepathic transfer being in some way comparable to radio broadcast and reception is the most popular theory of explaining ostensible mind-to-mind transmission; but in his article, "Models for the Explanation of Extrasensory Perception" (*International Journal of Neuropsychiatry*, Vol. 2, No. 5, October 1966), he argues that such a manner of explaining telepathy is only a model, not a theory.

"Basically," Dr. Tart writes, "the theory of mental radio postulates that the encoding mechanism is an electrical network in the brain which functions like a vacuum tube radio transmitter, feeding the human body as an antenna, just as commercial radio stations broadcast. The channel of transmission is then ordinary space. The decoder is an electrical network in the brain which functions like a vacuum tube receiver, again using the subject's body as an antenna."

Dr. Tart observes that such a conception of telepathy makes us feel comfortable and allows us to form familiar analogies. For example, subjects in telepathy experiments often have to get in the mood, just as the tubes in both transmitters and receivers have to "warm up" and stabilize their circuits before they function effectively. Some pairs of subjects work better together than others, as though they were transmitters and receivers which may establish contact only when tuned to the same frequency. In many instances, only certain elements of the target material is received, as if some kind of mental "static" has obliterated parts of the message.

However, Dr. Tart feels that the mental radio theory "fails miserably" on three important predictions: "First, it would predict a square-law falling off of telepathic effect with distance, which has not been observed. Second, it would predict that electromagnetic shielding of either agent [sender] or subject [receiver] should reduce or eliminate telepathic effects, but this has never been observed—indeed, there is some suggestion that shielding enhances the effect. Third, and finally, the known radiation of electromagnetic energy from the human body (primarily the brain waves or electro-encephalogram) is so weak with respect to the ambient noise level that exists on earth that it would be well-nigh impossible to conceive of an electronic instrument that could detect this radiation even a few inches from the head, much less at a distance of miles."

On the evening of November 13, 1970, as I sat chatting with Mrs. Ingrid Bergstrom and Mr. and Mrs. Gunnar Seaberg in the Marina Tower apartment of a Chicago-Toronto real estate man, Mrs. Bergstrom reached for a pad of paper and quickly wrote the number "564" on the top sheet.

"Let us call Olof to come in here," she laughed. "We will stump him." She tore the sheet from the pad, hid it under a sofa pillow.

Olof had been demonstrating a number of "psi" experiments to several men and women in an adjoining room, and his face seemed almost illumined as he joined us. Perhaps he thought he might obtain a moment or two of relaxation.

"Olof, quickly, tell us the number I have written on a sheet of paper," Ingrid demanded.

Olof's eyes widened slightly and the broad smile that had been curving his lips disappeared. "*Ja*, this is a number that you have written, Ingrid?" he asked.

"Yes, yes," Ingrid said. "I have told you that. Now do not hesitate. Tell us the number."

Olof sobered, turned to look at me from a distance of about six feet away. "Do you have this number in your mind, Brad?"

I visualized a bold "564"—large black numbers on a white background. "Yes," I said.

Then, without hesitation, Olof raised a finger toward Mrs. Bergstrom and told her: "Your number is *564*."

Did Olof Jonsson's brain actually probe my own, or did our two minds momentarily blend together and become one? Or could it be that on some transcendent level of consciousness our two minds are not really separate at all?

Dr. Stanley Krippner feels that, on the basis of telepathic evidence, the scientific establishment will eventually have to revise its image of man. Contemporary psychology and psychiatry, Dr. Krippner observes, view each person as an entity separated from everyone else, as an alienated being.

"Telepathy may teach us that in the basic fabric of life everything and everyone is linked, that man is continuously enmeshed, that he is always an integral part of all life on the face of the earth," Dr. Krippner states. "So far, the scientific establishment has ignored this possibility; it will, for one thing, refute many of their basic concepts."

Dr. S. G. Soal, the British researcher who conducted a series of classic tests with "mind readers," has written:

"In telepathic communication it is personality, or the linkage of personalities, which counts, and not spatial separation of bodies. This is what we might expect on the assumption that brains have spatial location and spatial extension, but that minds are not spatial entities at all.

"If this is true, then there is no sense in talking about the distance between two minds, and we must consider brains as focal points in space at which Mind produces physical manifestations in its interaction with matter."

Since January, 1970, Olof Jonsson has been teaching this elusive manifestation of mind to Len Donnells, a young engineer who works at the same Chicago firm that employs the psychic. On November 12, 1970, over cups of coffee in my room at the Pick-Congress, I asked Len how one went about learning telepathy from a master teacher. Olof Jonsson was also present, along with my friends Warren Smith and Glenn McWane. During the course of our rather lengthy interrogation, we sought to determine both what techniques might be utilized in teaching telepathy and what factors within a subject's personality might serve as determinants in whether he might be capable of learning telepathy, or any "psi" abilities.

"Len, when did you first become interested in ESP?" I asked.

Donnells: When Olof came to work at our firm about a year ago. I had never thought of ESP, let alone about developing it, but I had thought about developing better powers of concentration. I feel that concentration may be one of the greatest contributing elements in developing telepathy or clairvoyance.

Jonsson: Maybe together with meditation.

Donnells: This is what I'm trying to learn. I'm trying to mix the meditation with the concentration. To meditate and to concentrate, I think, are two different things. When you concentrate, you pick up throughts consciously. In meditation, I would say, it is your unconscious mind that does the concentrating.

"Don't you find it extremely difficult to cease conscious thinking and reach that plateau of readiness in your unconscious mind where telepathy and clairvoyance can work? Have you learned any mental aids that might help you to achieve this state?"

Donnells: Well, I can speak of an experience I once had with Olof. He picked a card at random from a regular fifty-two-card playing deck and asked me what I would like the card to be. "Would you like a picture card or a number card?" he asked. At that point I decided that I would try to guess it.

I had already learned that I must relax mentally as well as physically. I had found that even picking up a cup of coffee or lighting a cigarette can interfere, so now I thought only of cards. I let my mind try to hold every card that I could picture. After a few moments, I answered Olof and said that I wanted a picture card.

"Which picture card?" he asked.

I said a queen. Then Olof asked me which color, and I told him red; it is the queen of hearts. And that's what it was. It was as though something inside of me was telling me what to say. That's the hardest part to explain.

I have found a way to practice ESP, using the Zener deck with the five symbols. I have them sitting right on my desk, and I practice with them whenever I take a break. I have favorite symbols that I try to pick out. I decide on one symbol like the star, and I go through the cards until I feel that I really hold a star in my hand. I do this again and again.

"But what is it that tells you that you are correct?"

Donnells: I would say that when you work with the cards and relax your feelings and your thoughts, you quiet the domineering conscious mind and allow a higher level of mind to come into play. When I feel that I have a star in my hand and I feel that I am *really* certain that it's a star, the information is coming from another level in my mind.

"Why do you want to develop ESP, Len? Do you think that it might be of help to you in your work as an engineer? Do you think ESP would make you a more complete person? Why would anyone want to develop ESP?"

Donnells: In my case, call it pioneering, an inner sense of adventure. Some people are working with aereospace. In my position, how do I suddenly cease to be an engineer and become an astronaut? ESP is another great adventure into the unknown.

I have to tell you a very interesting thing that happened at the office when some of us were doing some experiments with Olof. This one fellow had called his wife just before the experiments, but after the tests had been completed, he walked to the telephone to call his wife again, forgetting that he just talked to her. Then he just stood there holding the receiver in his hand. He forgot what he was doing, who he was calling. He had to sit down and think a while to recall what he had been doing before the experiments.

Jonsson: I should explain that when we enter the state of meditation, we often go into some kind of trance. Higher senses begin to work, and we do not use our ordinary senses. We may not be aware of what is happening around us, and we may enter another dimension at that time.

"Had you inadvertently placed this fellow in an altered state of consciousness?"

Jonsson: Often when I do an experiment, these things happen spontaneously. We are not exactly the same until a minute or so after the tests have been completed. The trance is very light and we may still be aware of everything that happens around us. This is the way of meditation. Remember not to think. As soon as you start to think, you are guessing. State spontaneously what is in your mind.

"Len, do you feel that telepathy might be taught to people who are genuinely interested in psychic development. Or, could we, perhaps, take a class of enthusiastic junior high school students and teach them to be psychics?"

Donnells: Yes. As long as their heads are not too full of other thoughts and ideas.

Smith: Len, could you tell us something about your childhood? For example, did you have any serious childhood diseases? What kind of reading did you do?

Donnells: I had no serious childhood diseases and I read very little. Nature and the out-of-doors have always interested me. American history interests me. As a child I would often sit by myself a great deal and think.

Jonsson: Maybe you didn't know it at the time, but you were practicing a kind of meditation.

Donnells: I simply thought the typical thoughts of childhood. I thought about the future a great deal, which is normal for a child.

"When did you actively begin to study psychic development?"

Donnells: Within a week or so after meeting Olof and I learned what his abilities were. I have always been an open-minded person and I never condemn something which I have not seen for myself. When I witnessed Olof demonstrating ESP, I accepted the fact that this man had this ability, and that even if ESP might not work for me, my failure did not prove that it doesn't work for somebody else.

"And now that you have achieved a certain success in developing "psi" abilities, you feel that some delicate line between meditation and concentration may be the key to psychic development. You mentioned going through the ESP deck and trying to pick out your favorite symbols as a practice exercise. Is there any other developmental exercise that you have found helpful?"

Donnells: Well, quite by accident, I have found that perhaps certain *sounds* might unlock the unconscious mind. I am in the reserves and I recently took a military physical. The doctors were testing my hearing and I was sitting in a booth with soundproof earphones, listening to various tones. These tones start out very low—I guess they go on decibels—and they increase. When you hear the tone, you are to press the button and hold it down until you no longer hear the tone. They test first one ear, then the other. In both ears and at the same point, a certain tone at a certain amount of decibels relaxed me to the brink of sleep. This one certain tone just seemed to unlock a certain level of my mind and cause me to relax completely. I believe that one might be able to find a tone that could unlock the unconscious mind.

Jonsson: Of course. You can put someone to sleep with your voice. Certain notes of music can free one's psyche for meditation. Think of all those who use chants and mantras.

Smith: Olof, how would you teach someone to meditate?

Jonsson: The first step is to erase everything from your mind. Forget all about what you have been doing that day and try to relax your body.

Next, relax the nervous system. When you feel you have achieved a satisfactory level of relaxation, visualize an object, let's say something that you would like to buy for your wife.

Visualize, concentrate for a few moments, then forget it on the conscious level.

The forgetting is very important, otherwise you will draw the thought back to you.

When you get home tonight, ask your wife what present she would like to have you buy for her. If she names the object on which you meditated, you will know that you have been successful.

You might also try visualizing an item which you would like to have for dinner. While you are at work, relax, visualize the food, concentrate on it for a few moments, then forget it. If your wife serves that dish for dinner, you may chalk it up to coincidence the first time, but try it again. After a while, when you have achieved many successes, you may try visualizing some really exotic and unusual dish and experience the pleasure of having it awaiting you when you return home that night.

Smith: Would this work in a case where one might wish to change jobs?

Jonsson: It will work in any case. It can also earn you a raise!

Another device the beginner might find helpful is to fill a glass of water and place it on the table in front of him. He should stare at the water for five minutes and erase all thoughts from his mind. Don't think of anything. Just look at the water.

Take a pack of playing cards, shuffle them, select a card. Stare again at the water and see if you receive an image of the card. Turn the card over and check if you are correct. Practice this until you begin to score high in accuracy.

Once you have learned to do this effectively, you may consult the glass to gain more meaningful information. You may even practice precognition by looking at the water.

"Actually, Olof, isn't the water only a. . ."

Jonsson: An aid to help one relax. A physical object on which to focus one's attention and allow the unconscious to rise above the conscious mind. In learning meditation, the beginner often needs a crystal ball or some such physical device to aid him in achieving an altered state of consciousness. There are no magical properties in the glass of water or in the crystal ball. All higher knowledge comes from a transcendent level of our own minds.

Chapter Nine

TELEPATHIC HYPNOSIS

There is another facet of Olof's powers that may have awesome implications—that is his ability to control the actions of others. Telepathy has to enter into the manifestation of this eerie talent, or so it would seem to the mind that demands compartmentalization. We might term it telepathic-psychokinesis, or we might adjudge it as simply one shading of the spectrum of "psi" phenomena.

Whether this be psychokinesis or a telepathically implanted suggestion similar in nature to posthypnotic suggestion, Olof has been doing it for a long time. Here is a clipping from the Swedish newspaper *Varbergsposten*, reporting an experiment from the late 1940's:

> A young man put to sleep. . .at which time [he] spoke of many things and affairs which, humanly speaking, ought to have been hidden from him. Thus he gave accounts of certain events in the lives of those present which coincided astonishingly well. Engineer Jonsson also got the medium to play "Gubbe Nook" on a tonette and to strike up on the piano those melodies which the seance-participants wished to hear. The fact is that the young man in question can play neither the tonette or the piano.

The reader may smile and be satisfied that the above was

simply some kind of act prepared to confuse the gullible. But I am not so certain.

The first time that I witnessed one of Olof's demonstrations, he asked me to spread a deck of playing cards face-down on the table. I did so, expecting that he would then ask me to select a card and permit him to guess it as a test of his clairvoyance. Instead, he told me to pick all the fives out of the deck.

"Hey," I laughed, "you're the psychic. *You* pick all the fives out of the deck."

But Olof was adamant. He explained that he had been the object of test after test that evening. Now it was only fair that it should be someone else's turn. When I hesitated, he smiled broadly and said that he would help me out.

"I'll *need* your help," I protested. My secretary was laughing at my discomfort. Two brothers, both doctors in whose clinic we were meeting, stood by smiling their encouragement. Betty Jonsson commiserated by saying that Olof did things like this to her all the time.

"Now relax for a moment," Olof said. "Try to achieve a mood of complete calm."

It is the occupational hazard of the professional writer that his brain is perpetually flashing ideas and thoughts on and off, thus making tranquillity a mental plateau that is all too seldom attained.

But then my hand was moving over the spread deck, dipping here and there—first the five of diamonds, then the five of spades, then the five of clubs, then the five of hearts. I had selected the fives from a face down, spread-out deck of playing cards. But had it really been me who had performed this feat of mental magic against staggering physical odds?

"You did very well, Brad," Olof was laughing. "I think that you are very psychic. Let us now try another experiment."

He handed me a deck of twenty-five Zener ESP cards—the cross, the wavy lines, the square, the circle, the star—five symbols, five cards of each.

"Shuffle them, please," he bade me. "Now, after you have shuffled them thoroughly, place them behind your back and remove all the squares."

My newly achieved confidence was struck by instant self-doubt. "And you will help me?" I asked Olof.

He stood smiling beneath a diagram of the human nervous system that hung against a wall of the clinic.

"I will help you," he promised.

I put the cards behind my back, continuing to shuffle them rather clumsily. I certainly was not aware of any alien intelligence invading my own. I did not feel any sensation of hot or cold as another mind blended with mine in some kind of cosmic harmony. I certainly did not feel controlled. But the right hand that I have come to know and trust *was* the one that selected the squares, one by one, from the pack of Zener cards that my left hand held behind my back.

One time when Olof was riding on a Chicago bus on Clark Street with two friends, Sigge Rydberg and P. Hellman, Rydberg suggested an experiment.

"Olof," Rydberg smiled, "could you make the driver stop the bus right now in the middle of the block?"

"If he is susceptible, I can do it," Olof replied. He sat quietly for a moment, then smiled and nodded.

The bus driver slammed on his brakes so fast that Olof had to put out an arm to stop Rydberg and Hellman from falling forward. One fellow behind them said, "What's wrong with that crazy driver?" People throughout the bus were grumbling and complaining.

What did the bus driver say to the passengers?

"He didn't say anything," Olof recalled. "He seemed very confused. He just sat there for a few moments, then he started up again. What I had done was something like implanting a posthypnotic suggestion in his mind."

I asked Mrs. Ingrid Bergstrom, who, at the time of Olof's bus "experiments," had owned Verdandi's restaurant in Chicago, if she had ever seen Olof stop a bus.

"Oh, *ja*," she laughed. "He has done this several times to bus drivers when they are susceptible. Sometimes he has made them go past their stops. They pass the stop, then they halt half a block later right in the middle of the block. One time he made a bus driver make a U-turn and go around the block in the wrong direction."

On October 4, 1970, my wife and I were invited to brunch at the country home of Chicago architect Cary Caraway in Spring Green, Wisconsin. Among the guests were Olof and Betty Jonsson and Wes and Svetlana Stalin Peters.

After witnessing several demonstrations of Olof's telepathic ability, Svetlana furrowed her brow and seemed to suppress a slight shudder. "But could this ESP be used to control others?" she wanted to know. "Could it enter another's mind and dominate his thoughts? I am afraid of anything that might rob another of his free will."

Later, I asked Olof if he thought a powerful psychic sensitive could influence the thoughts and actions of others.

"Yes," he said, "I believe that this is very possible. If I concentrate, I can get a susceptible person to change his mind very easily. And if I work long enough with anyone, regardless of his resistance, I can change his mind.

"One time," Olof told me, by way of an example, "Betty did not wish to accompany me to visit some people to whom I thought it very important for her to be especially gracious. She told me that she would not meet these people for anything in the world. I simply said, 'Very well,' then I went into another room and began to concentrate. I blocked out what she had in her mind and put in its place a great desire to meet those people. Five minutes later when I came back into the room, she told me that she had changed her mind. That night she was perfectly charming to the people, and no one could have guessed that earlier in the evening she had refused to accompany me to their home."

Olof reminded me of the time in Australia when he had stood in the audience and made a political speaker suddenly denounce himself and endorse his opponent. "And," he chuckled, "don't you remember when I caused you to wait in your home and ask us if we wanted some coffee?"

I did indeed. Once when Betty and Olof were driving from Harvey, Illinois, to spend a weekend at our home, I was in the process of leaving the house to drive to my office to address some envelopes before our guests' arrival. I stood in the doorway, then slipped off my coat and told my wife that I would have a Dr. Pepper in the kitchen because Olof and Betty would soon be arriving.

Within fifteen minutes, a familiar Ford with Illinois plates pulled up in front of our home in Decorah, Iowa. After we had exchanged greetings, I smiled and asked, "How about a cup of coffee?"

The laughter my offer provoked was out of all proportion to its basic potential. Sensing my confusion, Olof explained that a few miles out of town, he told Betty that he had received an image of me slipping on my coat and preparing to leave the house.

"I will tell him to wait, that we will be there in fifteen minutes," he said. "And I will tell him to offer us a cup of coffee as soon as we are inside."

"Oh, Olof," Betty cautioned him. "You know Brad doesn't drink coffee. A noncoffee drinker seldom thinks of asking anyone if he would like some coffee."

But I had indeed offered the travelers a cup of coffee the moment they had entered our living room. I do attempt to be the good host, but my standard offer is, "Would you like something to drink?"

Once again, as with my selecting the fives from a deck of playing cards or my fishing out all the squares from a Zener pack held behind my back, I was not the least aware of any outside force or intelligence compelling me to remove my coat and await my guests, nor did any mysterious voice whisper the command to pour the coffee for them upon their arrival. All of these actions seemed to be my own, done entirely of my own volition.

It is rather frightening if one really considers the implications of this strange facet of "psi," this "telepathic-psychokinesis," or whatever it may be. Perhaps there exist other masters of this awesome talent who are not as jovial and benign as Olof Jonsson. Maybe, down through the ages, this has been what black magic, voodoo, and hexing have really been all about—the genuine ability of one mind to affect the thoughts and the behavior patterns of another. Psychokinesis, the direct action of mind upon matter or mind upon mind, may be the real power behind what superstition and ignorance have termed the "Black Arts."

What lies ahead if man should seriously begin to cultivate and develop his own inner resources of psychic ability? Within the pages of this present volume, Olof Jonsson shall give us some rather clear prognostications of what we may expect in our evolutionary future; while at the same time, he indicates how the serious student may acquire many of these psychic benefits today.

Some years ago, Olof gave a demonstration of psychokinesis at a Rotary Club meeting in Lidkoping, Sweden. According to the local newspaper, the most remarkable experiment was this:

> An empty pilsner bottle was placed on a table in the middle of the room. One of the waiters of the hotel was called in and asked to seat himself on the floor a few yards from the table. On the other side of the table, three or four yards away, stood Jonsson. He concentrated awhile and held the palms of his hands high upward in the direction of the table. Then he took a couple of steps backward, and in the same instant, the bottle began to shuffle across the table as if dragged by an invisible hand and fell to the floor with a loud noise. A thorough investigation by those present eliminated all thought of trickery or bluff.

Professor Sune Stigsjoo from Goteborg, Sweden, told me that he considered Olof Jonsson foremost among today's psychic sensitives. Stigsjoo, today a publisher, recalled the demonstration Olof gave for the Rotary Club in Lidkoping and the remarks he made that evening as a speaker to supplement the psychic's experiments:

"The older scientists' belief that the limits of research have been reached are shown up now as an error. Science today expresses its distinct veto of our consistent materialism.

"Physics and philosophy have been brought into a closer relationship through twentieth century research, and mankind is able to discern the outlines of a fruitful search for truth. With good reason, we can speak of a new science—a new physics, a new biology, a new psychology. A completely new view of the nature of matter governs the new physics. Research into the nature of matter has, in our time, put an end to classical physics; matter has been analyzed out of existence. Matter has become something non-material, namely energy.

"We are facing a revolution in the definition of the nature of man. Parapsychology offers an area of research with the possibility of unheard-of consequences which may surpass every other science. However, just as chemistry was preceded by alchemy, parapsychology had, and still has, a marsh of superstition to fight its way through. But those scientists who wrestle with what we call psychic phenomena have become so moved by the perspective of the future that they, like Professor Lombroso, feel it their duty to science to take their stand fearlessly on the firing line for this new area of research."

In the course of this book, we shall take our place on the firing line, at the shoulder of a man who has been paranormally gifted since early childhood. We may be sniped at by skeptics and doubters who are reluctant to enter a dimly lighted territory which they do not understand. We shall have to be prepared to duck bricks and stones hurled by those who fear the Unknown and what it may represent. We shall never be able to leave our backs nor our flanks unprotected from the heavy fire which shall come from the defenders of orthodoxy, both scientific and theological, who condemn without fair trial that which they judge as both material and non-material heresy.

If such opposition does not deter you from this most remarkable quest, then come along. You may rest assured that you will never be disappointed.

Chapter Ten

THE STRANGE WORLD OF DREAMS

On his trip to the United States in 1953, Olof found that accounts of his psychic abilities were well known among the passengers aboard ship.

"Hey, Jonsson," one man approached him. "Look, all you have to do is just sit off to my side while we're playing cards. You know, give me a signal now and then, and we'll clean up. How would you like to dock a wealthy man, eh?"

"My talents are not to be employed in such a manner, sir," Olof told the gambler, moving along the deck as rapidly as he could.

"We've heard a great deal about your exploits in Scandinavia," an obviously wealthly tycoon told him over dinner one evening. Waving aside Olof's modest protestations, the man offered him a long cigar. He frowned at Olof's polite refusal, then put an arm around the Swede and led him out on deck.

"Look, Jonsson," he said, affecting a tone of earnest fellowship. "I'm going to come straight to the point. I've never really believed in this ESP junk and ghosts and things until we started hearing all those stories about you in Denmark and Sweden. And now after watching your experiments tonight, well, I have to say that I'm much more open-minded now.

"You see," he went on in a low whisper, "I had to do quite a bit of business while we were in Rome, you know, just before we came up to Copenhagen and Sweden, and, ah, I had to leave my wife alone quite a bit. And, ah, well, you hear all these stories about these gigolos and wealthy American wives. . . ."

"I'm sorry, sir," Olof said, shrugging off the man's arm. "I do not use my abilities to spy on people's private lives or to keep an eye on a wife's fidelity."

As Olof hurried back to the dining room, he heard the man snort after him: "I had him figured for a phoney!"

In order to avoid unintentionally involving himself in a shipboard imbroglio, Olof began to spend more and more time in the company of an elderly dowager who enjoyed having Olof demonstrate his "psi" abilities for her and her friends. Although the woman was terribly absentminded and would often introduce Olof to the same people twice in the same afternoon and insist that they watch a demonstration similar to one they had observed only an hour before, the Swedish psychic found her erratic company preferable to that of gamblers and suspicious husbands.

One morning Olof found his elderly friend completely distraught and alternately weeping disconsolately and cursing the ship's crew indiscriminately. When he at last managed to calm her, he learned that she had lost an expensive necklace and some heirloom rings.

"They're gone," she wailed, "stolen from my room. This isn't a pleasure vessel, this is a pirate ship!"

Later that day, Olof was summoned to the captain's quarters. "Jonsson," the captain told him, "we've searched everywhere and questioned all of the men. We cannot find that woman's jewelry anywhere. She's a wealthy woman, and eccentric though she may be, she has powerful and influential friends. If she continues to suggest that this line is managed by a bunch of pirates, the publicity will not do us any good."

"How valuable are the pieces?" Olof wanted to know.

"Very," the captain said, biting down on his pipe stem. "I tried my best to persuade her to place them in the ship's safe as soon as she came on board, but she wouldn't hear of parting with them for even a moment. She said she didn't trust our safe.

Now she holds me personally responsible. Jonsson, can you help us?"

Olof replied that he would certainly do whatever he could, then left the captain to chew nervously on his pipe stem. Although he had promised a group of newfound acquaintances that he would join them for a game of shuffleboard, the psychic decided that missing jewels must take precedence over deck sports.

"I went back to my cabin," Olof recalled recently, "and induced a dream state. Since I am able to control my dreams, I concentrated for a few moments on the woman's jewelry, then I allowed my conscious mind to slip into light sleep in order to permit a transcendent level of mind to provide me with a 'dream' of where the jewels lay."

In his dream, Olof saw his elderly friend hiding her valuable necklace and rings in a green glove, which, in turn, she hid amidst her luggage. Upon his awakening, it became clear to the psychic that her mistrust of the ship's safe had prompted her to safeguard her treasures according to her own measures. But, then, after taking such pains, she had forgotten all about their secret storage place.

In order to avoid possible embarrassment, Olof suggested that the captain have his officers once again gain permission to search the dowager's quarters, looking carefully for the green glove amid her luggage. Later that afternoon, Olof received a report that the necklace and the rings had been found precisely where he had "dreamed" that they would be.

On the following morning, Olof stood at the railing of the ship, bidding a good-morning to the Statue of Liberty.

"Oh, Mr. Jonsson," the dowager called to him from her deckchair, "I do hope that you will have an enjoyable and profitable future in our United States."

Olof expressed his thanks for her sentiments, turned to look back at the New York skyline.

"Oh, Mr. Jonsson," she called again. "I must tell you that my precious possessions were returned to me. Because of the great relief I enjoyed at having them brought back to me, I went to bed and slept like I have not slept in ages. I slept so well that I had a beautiful dream that told of many wonderful things that

are about to happen to me. Tell me, Mr. Jonsson," she wanted
to know. "Do you believe in dreams?"

"I do on occasion, Madame," Olof smiled. "Sometimes, I
have heard it said it is possible that dreams may even come
true."

*The many types of dreams belong among the strangest
manifestations of the human life-rhythm. Some people seldom
remember their dreams, while others, night after night, experience the most dramatic scenes of ghost-ridden realities. There
are calm dreams, restful dreams, and terrible nightmares which
can etch themselves so vividly into one's mind that he will
always carry their memory.*

*The eminent doctor Paul Bjerre has devoted a great deal of
research to dream investigation and interpretation. In his book,*
The Healing Power of Dreams, *Dr. Bjerre poses fascinating
questions about the conflict between the conscious and the
unconscious.*

*I agree with Dr. Bjerre when he theorizes that the uncon-
scious is our connection to the cosmic, the universal, while our
conscious mind is concerned with our striving to embrace what
is happening around us, to make it our own, and to impose on it
our individual stamp. It seems quite clear that each individual
life hangs in suspension between these two opposite viewpoints.*

*If man truly desires to reach the ultimate, he must at some
time convert himself into a passive riverbed and allow his
independent spirit to become part of the universal flow of life.
At the same time, he must feel that he has the power to
manifest that universal flow of life in the physical body that
bears his name and his personality. As human beings on the
earth plane, we must appreciate our being anchored in the Earth
as an essential element of the Cosmos which lies closest to us.
Yet, at the same time, we know that we have the ability to
ascend freely toward the dimensions of light and warmth which
revolve around us.*

*Whenever one speaks of dreams, he will soon offer accounts
of ones which have come true. Nearly every person with a
normal dream life has quite probably, at one time or another,
dreamed something that eventually came to pass. I think that*

everyone could supply several examples if he were sufficiently foresighted to set down his dreams immediately upon awakening each morning. A periodic reference to these notes and synopses of dreams would indicate that he has obtained glimpses of the future during more than one evening.

Dreams are like rivers, and they flow out of our conscious minds much too quickly. He who would study his ability as a dreamer of precognitive dreams would be wise to put a pad and pen by his pillow, so that he may immediately make notes on his dreams—even if he should chance to awaken during the night.

Many times in my dreams I have seen rail disasters, sea tragedies, and airliner crashes. I have heard terrible explosions, followed by dreadful screams and cries. I have seen stretchers bearing away the injured and the dying. When I awaken the next morning, the newspapers and the broadcast media carry the same pictures of the accidents that I saw the night before.

Olof Jonsson believes that each individual may probe his own dream life to find solutions to the most crucial problems in life, provided by his unconscious. Once one has learned to mine the psychic wealth of his dreams in this manner, Olof maintains, he will acquire a daily consciousness that will make his own life harmonious and his interaction with others much happier.

Dr. Stanley Krippner, Director of the Dream Laboratory at the Maimonides Medical Center in Brooklyn, New York, also feels that one may gain a greater insight to his inner life and, thereby, become a more sensitive, full-functioning individual, merely by paying attention to his dreams. Dr. Krippner has offered a number of specific suggestions to help one recall dreams, among which are the following:

1) When you first awaken in the morning, don't jump out of bed. Let your mind dwell on the first thing that pops into it. Try to think only of this one thing for a while. Do not let daytime interests interrupt just yet. If you are lucky, you may find that this first waking thought actually has something to do with your last dream before awakening. It may suddenly remind you of the contents of the dream. Usually the whole dream will come to you in a flash. You may have to try this technique several mornings in a row before getting results.

2) Keep a notebook of dreams you do remember. Look for

important ideas or themes. You may find that a certain topic comes up again and again. Perhaps you have been working on a problem at night without being aware of it. You can discover how your daytime actions have affected your dream themes. You may even find cases in which your dreams have suggested actions you actually were able to carry out later!

3) Look for items in your dreams that might be symbolic of something else. Do you dream of wise old men, kings, queens, bridges, rivers, unusual animals? What do you think these items symbolize? Avoid making hard and fast judgments. Get the opinion of your family and your friends. Without a skilled analyst, it is unlikely that your judgment will be correct. In other words, it is more important that you enjoy the dream than that you correctly analyze it. Get into the habit of appreciating your dreams rather than attempting to become an amateur psychoanalyst.

4) Look for puns in your dreams—a play on words, a play on numbers. Word puns are common and often can be discovered. In one dream, for instance, you could be very *bored* while staring at a blackboard; if the blackboard scene occurs while you are talking to a particular person, it might indicate that you really think of that person as boring.

5) Before going to sleep, review the work you have done on a problem or a question which has you stumped. If necessary, concentrate several evenings in a row. If you have given the problem enough attention, you may find that unconsciously you will work the problem out. In the morning, you may remember a dream in which the solution or possible solutions to your problem appeared. This is one way of actually encouraging creative dreams to occur.

6) Keep dream diaries over a period of time. Record your dreams for six months or a year. Have other members of your family or your friends do the same. Determine as best you can, which dreams reflect personal problems, which dreams involve national or international events, which are creative, and which are symbolic.*

*Steiger, Brad. "How Science Is Unlocking the Mystery of Your Dreams." *Family Weekly,* January 12, 1969.

Chapter Eleven

MIND TRAVELING ON OTHER PLANES OF BEING

I have long nurtured an interest in what is commonly known as "astral projection," perhaps more properly termed "out-of-body experience" by the parapsychologists. Whatever term one chooses, he is generally referring to those instances in which the spirit—the mind, the soul, or whatever one elects to name the very essence of man—has been somehow freed from the physical confines of the body and has soared across the city, across the transcendent boundaries of other dimensions, or merely across the room to bob about at the ceiling. Most people who bother to think about such experiences at all usually associate such dissociation of body and soul with the moment of physical death. But the special element in an out-of-body experience is the fact that the soul is able to return to the physical body with conscious memories of the ethereal excursion. Indeed, this essential factor makes the whole transcendental act an experience, rather than a conclusion.

For those who steadfastly deny the existence of a soul, no amount of empirical evidence can convince them that men and women who have claimed out-of-body projection during times of acute pain, sorrow, illness, or fatigue were not hallucinating. For those who do accept the concept of the soul, but are convinced that the essential spirit and the flesh are unable to separate until the moment of physical death, research in the area of out-of-body experience tends to border on the blasphemous. For those who do accept the possibility of out-of-body experience, but are quite certain that it is but a facet of "psi" phenomena, such as "traveling clairvoyance," the claims of one who is adept at freeing his soul from his physical shell tend to rest on the "wrong" side of the amorphous, but stoutly maintained, line of demarcation that separates *occultism* from *psychical research.*

In my opinion, there seem to be at least seven types of spontaneous, or involuntary, out-of-body experiences:

1) Projections which occur while the subject sleeps.

2) Projections which occur while the subject is undergoing surgery, childbirth, tooth extraction, etc.

3) Projections which occur at the time of accident, during which the subject suffers a violent physical jolt which seems, literally, to catapult his spirit from his physical body;

4) Projections which occur during intense physical pain.

5) Projections which occur during acute illness.

6) Projections which occur during pseudo-death, wherein the subject is revived and returned to life through heart massage or other medical means.

7) Projections which occur at the moment of physical death when the deceased subject appears to a living percipient with whom he has had a close emotional link.

In addition to these spontaneous, involuntary experiences, there also seem to be those voluntary and conscious projections during which the subject deliberately endeavors to free his essential self from his physical body.

Dr. Eugene E. Bernard told Thomas Leach of the *Chicago American Magazine* that on the basis of his preliminary research, he would estimate that one out of every hundred persons has experienced some sort of out-of-body projection. Dr. Bernard stated that his study indicated that such projections occurred most often "...during time of stress; during natural childbirth; during minor surgery; and at times of extreme fear." In addition to these spontaneous instances, Dr. Bernard admitted that he had also encountered a number of "old pros," who seemed to be able to have out-of-body projection almost at will.

Olof Jonsson is such an "old pro."

"In the midst of parapsychological investigators, I have succeeded in setting free my astral body," Olof agreed. "I have been able to give an account of happenings which were occurring at other locations at the same moment that my physical body sat under strict control. All these experiments in out-of-body projection have been carefully controlled, and my reports have been proved to have agreed with distant events. It has happened that a faint figure of my astral body, easily identifiable as me, has been caught on film."

When I pressed for more information of such a startling bit of substantiating evidence—a photograph of a "living ghost"—Olof shook his head sadly. "The professor who took the picture died just a few years ago, and his wife, who had always detested his interest in parapsychology, burned all of his books, notes, and effects. But some day, when the conditions are harmonious, I will do it again, *ja*."

Although that precious photograph no longer exists, a Swedish doctor, whom we shall name Dr. Carlsborg, testified that an image of Olof Jonsson once appeared in his home in Malmo. According to Dr. Carlsborg:

"I met Olof Jonsson at a friend's party and immediately, and perhaps rudely, I expressed my skepticism. Although Jonsson had never been in my home, he went into what appeared to be a very light trance and described numerous particulars in my residence. When he described the children's bedroom, I began to lose my skepticism, but when he went on to describe the children and give their names and ages, I became quite convinced of his abilities.

"One night some weeks after Olof had visited my home to verify his impressions and to meet my family, I was disturbed from my reading in the front room by my daughter's delighted laughter. I hurried to her bedroom to inquire after her, since it was past her bedtime. When I asked her what had amused her so, she replied: 'Oh, Father, that nice Engineer Jonsson was here smiling at us.'

"I telephoned Jonsson's apartment, but there was no answer.

When I at last was able to contact him, I said: 'I understand that you carried on an experiment with us tonight. My daughter saw you plainly in her bedroom where she and her brother sat reading.'

"Jonsson admitted that he had been sitting in a theater earlier that evening, waiting for a somewhat uninteresting film to run its course. Since his companion found the film fascinating, while Jonsson was bored, he decided to turn off his conscious mind and allow his astral self to wander. For some reason he had found himself in our home, smiling at my daughter and son, who were both seated in their bedroom, reading."

"Olof, how can you control such a thing as astral projection, out-of-body experience?" I asked.

Jonsson: I can control such projection with my mind. First, I either lie on a couch or sit in a chair. Then I close my eyes and I concentrate on being outside of my body, looking at myself lying there. I *think* myself out of my body.

"You actually will yourself out of the body?"

Jonsson: Yes. I do this by concentrating on being outside of my body, looking at myself. After a couple of minutes, I can see myself lying there. Once I am free of my body, I think of all the different places I would like to visit—Malmo, Stockholm, Copenhagen—and then I wish me there. When I think of Malmo, the scenery just changes, and I am there. I can see the people around me, but they cannot see me. I can just walk around unencumbered.

"Do you ever experience a rushing sensation or see multi-colored lights?"

Jonsson: No, nothing. I just feel completely harmonious. . . at one with the universe. I am in my *real* body, not my sluggish, physical shell.

When I am doing astral projection, it is a very happy time in my life. I do not miss the earthly life at all. The cares and considerations of the physical plane mean absolutely nothing to one who is in his astral body. The Earth dimension does not mean one thing to him.

"Do you think that is what it will be like for you when you

make the final projection, the final separation of mind from body?"

Jonsson: Yes, I believe so. That final separation should be the happiest time in one's existence.

Psychical researcher Frederic W. H. Myers believed out-of-body experiences to be the most extraordinary achievement of the human will. "What can be a more central action—more manifestly the outcome of whatsoever is deepest and most unitary in man's whole being? Of all vital phenomena, I say, this is the most significant; this self-projection is the one definite act which it seems as though a man might perform equally well before and after bodily death."

Dr. Hornel Hart's investigation of out-of-body experience and "psi" phenomena led him to theorize that the brain was but an instrument by which consciousness expresses itself, rather than a generator which produces consciousness. Dr. Hart contended that the available evidence strongly supported the testimonies of those individuals who maintain that the essence of personal consciousness might observe and act at long distances away from the brain.

Olof Jonsson's method of achieving voluntary out-of-body projection:

I lie down in a comfortable position, close my eyes, and relax until I reach the stage between waking and sleeping. Even though I am now into this hazy, in-between zone of consciousness, I still have full control over my mind.

After a few moments, I begin to visualize myself outside of my body. Once one has become adept at astral projection, it takes no more than a matter of seconds until one's spiritual essence is floating above the physical body. When my astral self has been freed, I then visualize where I would like to be, and I am there, instantly.

It seems easier to visit family and friends when one is in the astral body. It appears quite evident that there exists some kind of force there to help draw one back.

Hypnosis can be helpful in freeing the neophyte astral

traveler from his body, but this method should be considered only if a good professional hypnotist of high repute and extensive experience in such matters is available.

"I have learned a great deal from my personal out-of-body experiences," Olof once reflected. "I have never used this ability to spy upon others or to attempt to learn things which others have decided to keep from me. And you can imagine how many times a man or woman has approached me to help them keep watch over the intimate lives of their spouses in order to gain evidence of disloyalty. I have never involved myself in such matters.

"No, what I have gained from astral projection is that calm and peace that can only come from being in harmony with the Universe. I have learned to place the value of my fleshly body in its true perspective, and I have come to realize that the concerns and cares of the Earth plane are very insignificant indeed. To be free of the flesh, to soar to other cities and countries completely unencumbered by Time and Space—what a happy thing!"

Chapter Twelve

RECREATING THE PAST WITH PSYCHOMETRY

If the past completely ceased to exist, we should have no memory of it. Yet each of us has a large and varied memory bank. Therefore, the past must exist in some sense; perhaps not as a physical or material reality, but in some sphere of its own. The transcendent level of consciousness does not differentiate between past, present, and future, but is aware of all spheres of time as part of an "Eternal Now."

Knowledge of some past event or personality acquired through other than normal sensory channels or inference based on sensory data is said to have been gained through *retrocognition.*

Olof Jonsson has said that he is able to relive the past most easily through the "psi" ability known as psychometry.

Psychometry, simply stated, means that a medium or sensitive can read the history of an object that he holds in his hand. People who had something important to do with the object a long time ago are "called forth" by the medium and are portrayed as they lived at that time. In some cases, the medium can hear music that had some connection with the object.

I have seen hypnotists obtain good psychometric results from "ordinary" subjects in the hypnotic trance state. Some mediums go into full trance when they practice psychometry, and others remain fully conscious.

For my part, I achieve the best results and the strongest impressions when I am in a half-trance, with my immediate surroundings completely shut out. When the impressions come streaming in, I feel as though I was actually fully present where the happenings related to the object took place. I may find myself in a strange city in the midst of strange people. I may hear songs, music, and foreign languages being spoken. Sometimes while psychometrizing an object, I may be transported several centuries into the past and receive a true picture of the daily life and courses of events of an earlier time.

Once, at a seance in Stockholm, a woman asked if I might be able to tell her something about her brother by holding a letter that he had written. No member of the family had heard from him for nearly a decade. Almost at once, as I held the letter, I was following a man whom I knew somehow to be her brother. I described his involvement in a desperate act, which his sister later verified. I saw him boarding a passenger ship for the United States, and I knew that this letter had been written shortly before he embarked on his voyage. The young man became extremely depressed, then physically ill. I could clearly see that he fell in with bad companions on board ship and was murdered soon after his immigration to the United States.

Not long ago, here in Chicago, a businessman handed me a package and challenged me to tell him what was inside. I had not held the package long when I received several very disagreeable impressions. I heard a particular strain of martial music that the world has been gratefully free of for a few years. I heard raised and shouting voices sounding in unison. I saw death, terrible destruction, concentration camps.

"Hitler," I said. "Whatever is in here belonged to Adolf Hitler." And then I saw a clear impression. "It is an ashtray. An ashtray that belonged to Hitler." And that is exactly what it was.

In my experience, it is more difficult to draw impressions from letters and written materials than from personal ornaments which have adorned the subject's body. Rings, brooches, necklaces, bracelets, and the like, seem to have a special way of storing impressions from the wearer. The individual revelations received from such objects can, in an astounding manner, be a mirror of the wearer's character and his involvement in past events. By holding a person's ring, pen, or watch in my hand, I have been able to make very accurate appraisals of character.

Ingrid Bergstrom: (Holding up a square of checked cloth in a large frame) This is a little tablecloth to be used on a nightstand. I got it from my aunt, and she, in turn, got it from her sister-in-law, who worked for the King of Sweden for thirty years.

"And you decided that you would use the tablecloth to test Olof?"

Mrs. Bergstrom: *Ja,* I always like to have proof of his powers. As long as I have known Olof, I still like to continue to test him to be certain that he is not just lucky.

But when you look at this piece of cloth, could you say that it had been in the castle of King Gustav V any more than you could say that it had been in the Salvation Army store, or any one of a thousand places?

"No, there's not even a clue that it might have come from Sweden. It is just a simple checked tablecloth."

Mrs. Bergstrom: But even though I wanted to test Olof again, I wanted to do it without anyone around who would laugh at him, because I respect him. He is a very fine man. So one day at Verdandi's, he came in and I thought that I would have a cup of coffee with Olof while he was eating, and then I would ask him to tell me about the tablecloth. If he makes a mistake, nobody will know about it but me. Nobody will laugh. But if he is good, I thought next, no one can testify that he was correct. I told Ola, the waitress, to be around the table just in case Olof would say something.

So I sat down beside him and said, "Olof, I have something here. I would like you to feel it and look at it and tell me about it." Ola stood beside the table, smiling, looking over Olof's shoulder.

Olof took the cloth in his fingers, feeling it. I thought to myself: he's nervous; he can't keep his fingers still. Then he said: "Now I think I can tell you something about this. I see a large V. It is a very old man who had this tablecloth. And there is an old lady close to this. And a very big house. Very big."

And Olof kept making a big V with his fingers on the cloth. Then he looked at me and said: "I have a feeling that it came from a castle. Can you tell me what Prince Bertile had to do with this cloth?"

Then I gave up, for the tablecloth had belonged to Gustav V, the grandfather of Prince Bertile.

My secretary, Jeanyne Bezoier, took notes on a psychometric reading which Olof Jonsson gave her in the summer of 1969.

"I removed a gold necklace, which I wear for psychic protection and have seldom taken off since it was given to me three years ago, and offered it to Olof," Jeanyne recalled. "He rubbed the pendant between his thumb and forefinger for several moments, then gave me the following reading."

This was given to you by a young man who spent a great deal of time in Mexico and Yucatan. This necklace came from Yucatan. (Jeanyne: This was correct. B. K. had acquired this necklace in Yucatan.)

You observed some kind of ceremony when you received this necklace. (Jeanyne: I offered the necklace three times to the ocean, allowing the waves to rush over it, then I slipped the wet and cold necklace over my head.)

You love the ocean and water. (Jeanyne: I have a real thing about the ocean, especially the Atlantic.)

I feel sadness with this necklace. (Jeanyne: I rejected this impression, until I realized that, when sad or depressed, I have the habit of pressing the medallion against my cheek for comfort.)

I see a medium-sized woman in her early forties. She has dark hair, flecked with gray.... (Jeanyne: Olof went on to describe my mother in great physical detail.)

This woman is very open to psychism, but she has never expressed this interest because of her strict and orthodox rearing. She could be an excellent medium. (Jeanyne: Mother had received a strict and traditional German-Lutheran upbringing and I had never heard her express an interest in psychism. Later, when I confronted her with Olof's comments, she admitted a strong, but hitherto suppressed, interest in the psychic field. She had always been specifically interested in the "other side" and in mediumistic phenomena. Another point of great interest is that at approximately that moment when I was receiving the reading in Chicago, my mother, in Minneapolis, was thinking about me and envying my attendance at what she believed was a seance.)

You have an older brother who is also very interested in the occult. (Jeanyne: Dolph has been interested in the occult since his early teens and was largely responsible for generating my own early interest in psychism.)

Tonight, I think, your parents are attending the theater. (Jeanyne: It was later established that my parents were, at the time of my reading, attending the theater in Minneapolis. After these preliminary comments, Olof presented me with many details of my emotional, mental, and physical condition and made some personal predictions for my future.)

From an examination of the notes of Olof's psychometric reading of Jeanyne's necklace, it should be obvious to the reader that "psi" phenomena do not obey rigid restrictions and that there is a great deal of psychic overlap in the exercise of any "psi" ability. When Olof touched Jeanyne's medallion, he not only "saw" her present condition, but he also had a picture of what she had experienced, and, perhaps, a clear view of her future.

The object which the sensitive requests in a psychometric reading may only be a tangible symbol of the bond between psychic and subject that the psychic feels is essential in order to get "in tune" with his client. It seems to me that psychometry is but a shading of clairvoyance, and once the sensitive's psyche has become independent of Time and Space, it is as likely to receive an impression of a future condition as it is an impression of the present or the past. It is my opinion that any kind of dogma fails when dealing with the phenomena which we have currently, for lack of a better term, grouped together as "extrasensory"; therefore, one is better off grouping all the individual facets of the transcendental mind under the blanket category of "psi," rather than splintering them off into separate compartments and ability groupings. As humans, we seem always compelled to brand the infinite with our finite stamp.

Chapter Thirteen

EMPLOYING PSI AGAINST CRIME

Although Olof Jonsson vowed never again to become involved in crimes of violence after the case of Officer Hedin
and the Tjornarp murders, he has been prevailed upon time and
time again to assist police authorities in solving murders,
kidnappings, and robberies. Jonsson much prefers to aid in
locating missing persons, for in the majority of such cases, he
has found that the loved ones are alive and have been purposely
hiding because of some pique or domestic misunderstanding.

In August, 1966, Olof Jonsson volunteered his psychic
services to the authorities who had been searching since July 2
for three young Chicago-area women who had disappeared on a
trip to the Indiana dunes region. Mrs. Renee Bruhl, Patricia
Blough, and Ann Miller were reported missing after some of
their personal belongings and Miss Miller's automobile were
found abandoned at the dunes park. An extensive air, lake, and
ground search had failed to turn up any sign of the young
women or any evidence that they may have drowned or met
with foul play.

By mid-August, authorities had begun to work on new leads
which indicated that the three women might have carefully
planned and executed their own disappearances. According to
the *Chicago Sun-Times* (August 27, 1966), Olof Jonsson was an

important factor in convincing investigators to dismiss theories of kidnapping and murder and to consider the three women as runaways:

Jonsson . . .said he was sure the girls were in Saugatuck and that they had bleached their hair and changed hair styles.

On July 29, Indiana police went to Saugatuck, and, after questioning waitresses, bartenders and horse stable owners . . .Sgt. Burke said there had been some identifications, but they were "not beyond doubt."

Jonsson was urged by Mr. and Mrs. Joseph Slunecko, parents of Renee Bruhl, to go himself to Saugatuck. He did so on August 14, in company with the Sluneckos and an Indiana state trooper. . . .

A waitress at the nightclub said that the night of July 30 . . . a customer called her attention to three girls sitting in a booth with a man . . . .The waitress went to the table and became convinced they were the girls whose pictures she had been shown, she said. In addition, she said, one of the girls addressed another as Pat.

Shown a recent unpublished photograph, the waitress said, "This is the girl they called Pat. What is her name?" It was a picture of Pat Blough.

The waitress noted that all three girls had bleached blonde hair, cut short.

At another night spot nearby, a doorman said he remembered checking the Illinois driver's license of a girl he said was named Ann Miller. . . .

Park Superintendent Svetic said of the identification in the Michigan resort, "It is a creditable identification of all three." He feels in his own mind, he said, that the sighting was creditable "not only because of the descriptions but because of the way they reacted when a waitress spent time at their table."

When I recently questioned Olof Jonsson about the case, he said that he had been given some cigarettes that the girls had left on the beach. "I saw at once that they were alive and that they had gone to Saugatuck. I was able to tell them many things about the girls and about their private lives. These things were not reported in the newspapers, and I must not mention them now. The girls have not yet been found, but I know they were alive at that time."

Olof does not limit his psychic sleuthing to police cases. As he has indicated on many occasions, he really prefers using his powers of mind to help people on an individual basis, and any time a friend is in need, Olof seems to know about it. Mrs. Bergstrom related such an instance:

"When I left Verdandi's that night, the safe was open," Ingrid Bergstrom remembered. "My husband, Gustav, was still in the restaurant, seeing to the details of closing for the evening, but I decided to go home. About two Gustav calls me and asks if I have seen our large wallet. Have I taken it from the safe? Have I hidden it? Am I playing a joke? I tell him that it was in the safe when I left. We know then that someone has stolen it."

Ingrid and Gustav searched their restaurant "downstairs, upstairs, in the office, wherever we could dream the money might be." Ingrid was a bit suspicious of one of the employees, but when she made even veiled references to his possible role in the wallet's disappearance he became highly indignant.

Finally, Ingrid turned to Gustav and said: "I wish I knew where Olle Jonsson is."

"Olle?" Gustav replied. "We haven't seen him for over a year."

"He lives now in Kenosha," Ingrid sighed. "If I knew his telephone number, I would call. I know that he could help us."

The next morning at eleven, Olof Jonsson stepped just inside the door of Verdandi's. "I know that you want to see me, and I know that you have lost something."

"Olof," Ingrid said, stepping out from behind the cash register. "Please come in."

"I'm sorry," Olof told her. "I have only a short time. I must meet Glenn Ford in just a few moments, and I have yet to go downtown."

"But, Olle," Ingrid protested. "Can't you stop in for just a moment? We must talk to you."

"I know that you have lost something," Olof said softly. "I have not yet concentrated to learn exactly what, but whatever it is, I will go into trance and I will see that you get it back. I will make the person who took it give it back to you."

Ingrid Bergstrom laughed at the memory of Olof's brusque assurance. "'Well, thanks a lot,' I thought. And Olof went right back out the door. He didn't even go back to Gustav's office to say hello."

But on the following morning when they opened their office door they found the wallet on Gustav's desk. Although they had not made a precise count of the money in the wallet before its disappearance, they both agreed that the four hundred dollars that had been returned with it seemed like an accurate figure.

Three weeks later, according to Ingrid Bergstrom, Olof Jonsson returned to Verdandi's. After the preliminary greetings, his first words were: "Well, did you get your wallet back?"

No one had told Olof that it had been a wallet that had been stolen from the Bergstroms, so Ingrid decided to learn just how good Olof Jonsson really was. "No," she lied. "I did not."

Olof's smile disappeared. "You didn't?" he asked incredulously. "But in trance I saw a white-haired man. It was the gentleman who works here cleaning floors. Anyway, I saw him with the wallet. I concentrated on him and made him feel so bad that he wanted to return the money at once. He had not spent any of the money, except one ten-dollar bill, so he used his key to get into the restaurant and return the money while you slept."

Ingrid confessed to Olof that his incredible clairvoyant ability had once again been true.

"We do not know whether the ten dollars was missing or not, because we had not made an accurate count of the money in the wallet before it was stolen," she told me. "But the old gentleman who cleaned up for us was never seen again by either of us after closing time the night before the money was returned. I suppose that one might argue that his conscience would have impelled him to return the money anyway, but I still think it was pretty good that Olof should know what had been taken from our restaurant, when it had been returned, and who had been the probable culprit."

Chapter Fourteen

"OLOF WANTED TO PLEASE"

In a letter to me dated November 9, 1970, Luke Salmon, an engineer with one of the nation's largest electronic firms, told of a number of attempts to measure Olof Jonsson's "psi" ability with sophisticated technical devices. I reproduce the letter with the writer's permission:

Dear Brad:

During a visit to Japan in March, 1970, I had the opportunity to have a pleasant conversation with a Dr. Motoyama, the head of the Institute of Religious Psychology in Tokyo. Dr. Motoyama has been making various physiological measurements, cardiovascular, respiration, galvanic skin resistance, and electroencephalograms with the purpose of determining if a man is sane, insane, or psychic.

Since my return to the U.S.A., I have requested and obtained permission from Dr. Motoyama to duplicate some of his experiments.

The method used to determine the mental state of a subject is primarily the analysis of a plethysmogram base line, in conjunction with galvanic skin resistance and respiration, simultaneously taken. If the base line of a plethysmogram is sinusoidal, with a high respiration rate, the indications are that the subject is insane. A plethysmogram base line that is sinusoidal, with a slow respiration rate, indicates that the subject is psychic. An almost straight plethysmogram base line, with a medium or normal respiration rate, indicates an average subject, stable, not hypersensitive, sane.

I am employed as an engineer in the electronic industry and am in no way medically or biologically oriented, yet the cybernetics involved are obvious and apparent. The whole method or system can be easily employed with a minimum amount of training.

Dr. Motoyama states that the autonomic nerves that control blood vessels contract or expand where the artery and the vein anastomose, increasing or decreasing the quantity of blood flow. The ordinary, normal person's autonomic nervous system works consistently at an even pace, stable, hence: an even, consistent blood flow and a relatively straight plethysmogram base line, with a normal respiration rate. The psychic person's autonomic nervous system pulsates at the respiration rate, causing the plethysmogram base line to pulsate likewise, appearing sinusoidal or wavy, at a slow respiration rate. Dr. Motoyama showed the graph of a schizophrenic, in which the plethysmogram base line was similar to the psychic's. However, the respiration rate was almost two times greater then the psychic's.

Cary Caraway and I made an attempt to make a plethysmogram of Olof. The attempt was not successful from the viewpoint of the type of plethysmogram we were looking for. *I believe that Olof can control the pen on the chart recorder:*

Olof did not know exactly what we were looking for. Olof was connected via a transducer to the strip chart recorder for the plethysmogram. In addition, he was also wired via electrodes (Lead I) to an oscilloscope for a electrocardiogram. The electrocardiogram was being taken for diversionary purposes, in the hope that Olof's attention would be on the oscilloscope trace, not the strip chart recorder that was monitoring and recording the plethysmogram. It became apparent that Olof could effect the movement of the recorder's pen. So, the question at this time is: Did Olof have an effect on the recorder's pen directly, or did Olof affect the recorder's pen indirectly by way of psychological, then physiological means?

The reason for using the diversionary tactics to throw Olof off the track of our actual purpose came about because of a previous occasion. When making an electrocardiogram on Olof, Cary and I asked Olof to increase his heart rate. The oscilloscope showed a change of 40 beats per minute (88 to 128) within a single trace sweep of 30 seconds! Prior to such an amazing feat, Olof appeared hesitant and wanted to know how the trace on the oscilloscope *should appear* for positive results. He was told that the rate was determined by counting the R portion [Lead 1] of the pulse. When the oscilloscope showed the increase in heart rate, there was a tremendous increase in noise level, obliterating P, Q, S and T segments, leaving only the R portion for counting the rate. Approximately 50% of the total trace amplitude was covered with noise.

Because of Olof's inquisitiveness in regard to the interpretation of the trace for count purposes, and because of the sudden increase in noise level, I suspect that Olof may not have increased his heart rate, but instead, somehow controlled the electron trace on the oscilloscope. During a conversation with Olof at a later date, he volunteered information relating to such a possibility, but hedged when asked if that is what he had done.

Additional testing under more controlled conditions must be done on Olof. How he made the heart rate change will be interesting to determine, regardless of whether he made the oscilloscope change or the heart rate change. I am not equipped with sufficient instrumentation to meter the psychic abilities of a man like Olof. It certainly would be interesting if Olof could be subjected to testing at Dr. Motoyama's Institute in Tokyo, where controlled test conditions and experienced personnel are constantly engaged in measuring subjects that have psychic ability.

For the ordinary psychic *(Olof is extraordinary),* Dr. Motoyama's system of measuring the autonomic nervous system via plethysmograms and respiration is excellent. The system is simple, inexpensive, and apparently reliable, depending on the experience of the data interpreter. It will allow the small, but interested, groups of psychic researchers to leave the realm of pseudo-science and gather data that can be meaningful when weighed. At this time, it is the only method I know for measuring a psychic.

Sincerely,
Luke Salmon

Shortly after receiving Luke Salmon's report, I had an opportunity to interview Salmon at length on the implications of such an accomplishment.

"Luke, exactly what is a plethysmograph?"

Luke Salmon: The plethysmograph measures the quantity of blood flow—not in pints, gallons, ounces, or grams, just in general quantity. Blood flow is usually measured at a finger or an ear. The gadget that I have is a U-shaped metal device with sort of a spring clip that will fit over the fingertip. Any finger will do. On the top part of the device, against the fingernail, is a little hole, and on top of the hole is a miniature light bulb. The light shines through the hole, going right through the fingernail and the finger. On the bottom of the finger, connected to this U-shaped device, is a photoelectric cell, which senses any change in light passing through the tip of the finger. Changes of light passing through the tip of the finger will occur due to volume density of blood that happens to be running through the tip of the finger. The volume changes as one's heart pulses.

"Then if I walked into the room and said 'free ice cream,' there would be lesser change in blood volume than if I walked into the room and told you, 'Your house is on fire.' Is that how it works?"

Salmon: No, probably the only thing the plethysmograph would show under such conditions is a change in heartbeat. You would be able to count these pulsations if your equipment was calibrated to determine the speed of the heart. The density of the volume of the blood would change more or less rapidly, depending on how you were stimulated.

The responses of the little photo cell goes to the Wheatstone bridge, an electronic circuit for when an imbalance occurs, and you can get a tremendous change in voltage. The resister, the photo cell, will keep changing and unbalancing the bridge as the blood varies.

But the area in which we're really interested from the psychic viewpoint is this: At the junction where anastomose occurs of an artery and a vein, there is a little muscle. This muscle is controlled by the autonomic nervous system. In the average person, the person who is not psychic, the muscle is pretty dormant. It doesn't move much. It is quite steady. It doesn't expand, it doesn't contract. As a result, the blood flow going through this area just makes its regular pulses, but it is not impeded by a contraction or an expansion of this muscle pressing against this area. Therefore, the base line of the plethysmogram will be straight.

The psychic and the insane have a rhythm of this muscle, contracting and expanding. So in addition to the pulse/heart rate going through this little junction, you will also see a second pulse. This we call a sinusoidal wave . . .and that will be shown at the baseline.

If, when you complete your plethysmogram, you should trace the peak at the bottom of the plethysmogram, you will see that you have another pulse in a person who is psychic or insane. As I explained, that additional pulse comes from the autonomic nervous system. The difference between the psychic and the insane person will usually lie in the slower respiration rate of the pyschic personality. Dr. Motoyama's examples were

10 for the psychic person, 19 for the insane person, with the normal person, 16.8.

"When you tested Olof, though, you felt that rather than controlling his heartbeat, he was controlling the movement of the machine."

Salmon: Yes. Going back a few weeks before we made this measurement, we ran an EKG on Olof, using an oscilloscope as the visual monitor and indicator. At that time, we asked Olof to increase his heartbeat. The EKG would, of course, measure his heartbeat. We used what we call a "lead one" connection, or configuration, and Olof was wired up with the electrodes. We had already told him how to count the pulses on the oscilloscope to determine what his heartbeat was. He had asked us, so we told him.

So then he said he was ready and at that time his heartbeat increased 40 beats a minute! It had been 88 and it went up to 128, and all within a 30-second period of time—or less! I couldn't measure the time element more closely because I was so shocked to see such a thing occur. It shouldn't occur. Not that fast. The best I can do is guarantee that it was under 30 seconds. It could have been 15 seconds, or 10 seconds, but I am certain it was under 30. It took a few seconds to gather my cool and start counting.

Another very significant thing occurred at the same time: The noise level increased to about 50% of the total trace, obliterating some of the important functions that normally take place in the heart which are easily read with an EKG. Prior to this rapid increase in noise, the noise level was acceptable and normal. But then, all of a sudden, there was this increase, which I can't account for at all. There were no loose wires, and Olof didn't move at all. He was completely relaxed.

"You didn't notice any facial contortion that might indicate emotional tension or . . .?"

Salmon: Possibly there was, but it would not have been responsible for that noise. You can stick your tongue out and yell, but it won't make any difference to an EKG. Only if you start moving your hands and shaking them. . . .

"But Olof's hands were stable?"

Salmon: Yes. So I suspected something unusual after our attempt at the EKG test. When I proceeded to make the plethysmogram measurement on Olof, I hooked him back up to the EKG again, like he was before, hoping to keep his attention on the oscilloscope and away from the plethysmogram. I didn't tell him how the plethysmogram was going to work, as I had told him how the oscilloscope would work. Olof would ask questions, but I would answer in technical jargon that wouldn't really tell him anything.

"Diversionary tactics."

Salmon: Yes, but then the pen began to make a lot of noise. It was ten-inch paper and the pen makes a long stroke. Soon Olof saw everyone looking at the plethysmograph chart recorder, so we told Olof what we were looking for. And then the pen began to go way up. I think Olof assumed that we wanted a broad stroke on the paper, but that is not the case—it's the *distances* between pulses that indicates heart rate.

"Olof wanted to please."

Salmon: Olof wanted to please, so he gave us a long stroke with the pen. Therefore, I wouldn't really count that as an accurate plethysmogram reading, but I would have to count it as a very significant reading of some sort! I don't know how he did it, but somehow, he controlled the pen. There's no way he could do it by affecting his blood rate that I can think of. Maybe it's possible, but it's really way out. I'd say he controlled the pen by psychokinesis.

In the introduction to the book *Behind the Curtain to the Unknown*, which he authored with the assistance of Berndt Hollsten, Olof dealt with the question of why the orthodox and the skeptical doubted and feared the claims of parapsychology:

> . . .One asks himself how it is that people in general show themselves to be so skeptical and derisive of everything that touches parapsychological phenomena and occult experiences. And yet it has been widely determined by so many tabulated areas of support that all doubt ought to be dispelled. Many highly reputed, pioneering scientists have defied public opinion and pledged their names and their honor in testimonials which should convince the skeptics.
>
> What can be the reason for this doubt of facts and realities that stamps the general attitude toward parapsychological phenomena?

Perhaps one comes closest to the truth by tracing the doubt to a competely simple confrontation with an apparition in full daylight, an experience which stimulates fear of an unpleasant awakening "behind the curtain to the Unknown," and echoes the fear of death which certain dogmatic religious creeds have instilled in modern man's subconscious. These impressions rise to the conscious surface with confusing thoughts of one or another forms of being coexisting with our own material sphere.

Occult phenomena need not necessarily be linked with ghostly phantoms out of a storehouse of fears; but, unfortunately, much too often, pure metaphysical phenomena have been mixed with what is commonly termed mysticism. Such a blending has made it difficult for people who do not clearly understand the reasons for such a mixture to be willing to accept anything at all that has to do with occultism.

...In spite of thousands of years of material and technological strides, we Westerners still stand at the starting point where contact with the source of life, the primitive cosmic force, is concerned....We are accustomed to think in terms of width, length and height. Certainly there are other dimensions which we so far have not discovered . . .When the nonmaterial strata have been investigated completely, parapsychological phenomena will come to be regarded as no more wonderful than many other areas of existence.

To a serious observer, a book of parapsychology may resemble most nearly a children's book of fairy tales. In such a way is this science characterized by the well-known researcher Dr. John Bjorkhem, who writes:

"They could sometimes come with great distortions of reality, but nevertheless, they inspired fantasy and stimulated the youthful joy of discovery in the unexplored land of probability. A miscellaneous item of science has its infancy as it derives knowledge and the inspiration for research out of fairy tales. Astronomy and chemistry would not be what they are today if certain learned men had not rummaged around to discover the foundations of astrology and alchemy.

"The parapsychologist on the whole has, perhaps, not gone so far beyond the fairy tale stage. He does not present claims and assertions; he still questions and tests. And he should not be forbidden that, for it is taking place under the broad heaven of the Faust-spirit."

"What do you think is the most important area that the parapsychologists might work in today?" I once asked him.

Jonsson: It seems to me that they feel clairvoyance seems most important to them.

Many scientists have told me, "Yes, it would be interesting to see you move the Prudential Building up into the air, but we are more interested if you can name fifteen cards out of twenty-five. Card-guessing means more to us because we can measure that."

They may be right in some ways, but not in others.

"What is your opinion of the environment of the laboratory?"

Jonsson: If the environment could be improved, I would agree that a laboratory would be the best place to do scientific testing. However, most labs do not encourage the right conditions for psychic phenomena.

In the first place, too many parapsychologists make the sensitive feel that they are more interested in what they might get out of him than they are in him as a human being. Some of them give the impression—and I know this is not their real thoughts—that they would gladly sacrifice a subject's complete energies, even his life, for science. I hasten to add that I, personally, have received good treatment at their hands. It seemed evident to me that they respected me very highly and that they thought highly of my abilities.

But it is so very important to create harmonious conditions, and most parapsychologists simply do not seem to recognize this. Too many researchers rush from one room to another. Maybe they do some office work for a few hours, then they rush down to test a medium with their minds occupied with all kinds of different things. They are not in any condition to conduct any kind of proper test.

In my opinion, the parapsychologists should have a number of informal meetings with the medium *before* the actual testing begins. They should grant enough time for the proper conditions to develop before they push a medium into an experiment. As it is now, too often the parapsychologist rushes in, chats briskly for three minutes, then plunges immediately into the experiment. There is simply no time for any kind of rapport to develop between the psychic and the researcher.

One time I drove to North Carolina, and it must have been midnight before I arrived at the university. I expected to be able to go to bed and rest, but the researcher said that he had some people coming to witness some experiments at once, and I was not able to go to bed until three in the morning.

"If you were allowed to dictate the conditions in the laboratories, how would you conduct ESP experiments?"

Jonsson: First of all, I would like the scientists to condition themselves with rest and meditation before the experiments, so that they were in a harmonious condition.

Next, I would like to be permitted to have some good "batteries" with me—that is, men and women with strong and positive vibrations. When you are sitting with a group of skeptical people, you feel their negativity very strongly, and it might take you a couple of days to get through to them so that you can conduct your experiments effectively. It is difficult to explain to certain scientists that you need a half hour, maybe more, to achieve the proper conditions—especially when too many of them make it clear that their patience extends not a second beyond five minutes.

At this writing, one of Olof Jonsson's lifelong dreams is in the process of achieving reality. A foundation has been established to enable Olof to devote more time to psychical research. Cary Caraway, Associate Architect, University of Illinois, serves as the president of the foundation, which, as Caraway explained, is incorporated in the state of Illinois under nonprofit corporate laws.

Over lunch at Chicago's Palmer House, I asked Caraway if he would tell me what "turned him on" to Olof Jonsson.

"We hired a technical engineer at the university who happened to have worked with Olof for about six months, and he told me about him," Caraway explained. "I had never been interested in ESP, although, of course, I was aware of the term and that other people were interested in the subject. From what this engineer told me, Olof seemed to be a psychic that was for real. So I made an introduction to meet him through this fellow."

Caraway had been advised not to initiate a discussion on ESP, but to allow Olof to bring up the subject. It took three luncheon dates before Olof brought out a deck of ESP cards.

"I had never seen such cards before," Caraway remembers, "and Olof asked me to try an experiment with him. As we did the experiment, I actually got a sensation of a tingling up and down my spine when he was transmitting the impression of a card to me. I had never before had such a sensation."

I wondered if Cary felt that his own ESP abilities had begun to develop since his meeting Olof.

"I wasn't even aware that I had any before I met Olof," he laughed, "but now I'm beginning to think that everybody has ESP in varying degrees."

What, I asked the president of the newly formed ESP Research Foundation, would they most like to accomplish?

"Number one, we would like to see Olof's abilities scientifically nailed down, so that 'psi' phenomena may be accepted in the scientific community," Caraway answered. "Number two, we would like to see if Olof can determine just how he does what he does and if he can discover a means to teach these techniques to others. If 'psi' abilities can be taught, then the gates are wide open to a remarkable future for everyone."

Chapter Fifteen

MASTER OF THE LAW OF GRAVITY

Olof Jonsson can stop a clock by looking at it. This unique accomplishment has nothing whatsoever to do with an unfortunate or unattractive arrangement of his facial features. On the contrary, if Olof were white-bearded and a bit stouter, he could pass as an excellent facsimile of a ruddy-cheeked Santa Claus. Olof's ability to halt the hands of a mechanical timepiece has to do with a remarkable psychic talent called psychokinesis, or telekinesis—the direct action of mind upon matter.

Swedish journalist Stig Arne Kjellen was sitting with Olof Jonsson in the Rainbow Restaurant in Stockholm in May, 1947, when he asked the psychic sensitive, mostly as a joke, whether, without moving from their table, he could take the cigar out of the mouth of a man seated across the dining room. Olof smiled and nodded his head. In the next instant, the cigar shot out of the man's mouth and landed in an ashtray at his side.

Kjellen reported that he had seldom seen a man so puzzled as the cigar smoker who had been momentarily robbed of his after-dinner pleasure. The journalist stated that he and Olof Jonsson were seated at least fifteen yards away from the target of their psychokinetic experiment.

"I have witnessed one hundred and forty principal telekinetic demonstrations by Olof Jonsson during which I have seen him move objects by sheer willpower," Kjellen said. "Those demonstrations which I have reported in the Swedish press were performed wholly and completely under the conditions upon which the controllers and I decided."

Kjellen cites one such demonstration when Olof was left in one room under strict control while other controllers entered an adjoining room. The sensitive had never been in either of the rooms; he had not even been in that particular home prior to the time of the experiment. The door to Olof's room was locked.

"A vase with four tulips was placed on a table in the middle of the room," Kjellen states. "Thirty seconds after Jonsson announced through the locked door that the test could be tried, we all saw the four tulips in the vase suddenly lifted to a height of approximately a yard and thereafter dropped down at various places in the room. The vase stood entirely undisturbed."

When the door to Jonsson's room was unlocked, it was determined through a comparison of notes with his controller that the psychic had not arisen from the chair placed in the middle of the room, but that he had looked sharply at the door until the moment that he had shouted that the test might begin. Coincident with his shout, the controller said, he had made a quick hand movement.

A second experiment was conducted that same day wherein a hyacinth was placed in a jar atop the same table. Olof was once again separated from the flower and locked in a room with a control.

"We heard Jonsson call, 'Be careful!' and at that moment the the hyacinth began moving," Kjellen declared in the July 21, 1959 issue of Home Journal. "The jar scraped against the saucer, and the hyacinth stalk made several small, rapid movements for seven seconds. Two hours later, the flower showed obvious signs of withering."

Kjellen has commented that he can testify to manifold examples of Olof Jonsson's remarkable psychokinetic abilities. "I have seen Jonsson lift flowers out of a vase while he stood more than three yards away," the journalist said. "Once the flowers were airborne, he spread them out like a fan as they moved across the room. I have seen him make a hanging lamp swing when he stood at a distance of four yards away."

Author Poul Thorsen has stated that he considers Olof Jonsson to be the only one of the numerous psychics whom he has met who can bring together *psychical* and *physical* phenomena. "Jonsson can perform the purely phenomenal, not to say the unbelievable, without falling into a trance and without spirit guides or other discernible trumpery making itself known. From my experiences, this is quite singular," Thorsen said.

In his book, *People's Unknown Capacities,* Thorsen recounts an evening of experiments with Jonsson wherein, "in an unmistakable way," Jonsson's astonishing clairvoyance manifested itself through psychokinesis. Certain answers were heard through knockings on a table that had been placed a couple of yards away from the psychic. "Jonsson produced fully-proved telekinesis, dictated by his clairvoyant insight, his subconscious, or more rightly said, his highly developed super-conscious," the author concluded.

In 1964, when Loyola University professor James Hurley was contemplating writing a book on ESP, he contacted Dr. Joseph B. Rhine, the dean of academic parapsychologists. Dr. Rhine told Hurley, "I find this man [Olof Jonsson] to be one of the finest sensitives I have ever tested."

As Hurley observes: "When you consider the hundreds of psychics Rhine has examined during the past three decades, the statement amounted to an accolade."

Dr. Rhine began his experimental laboratory work in psychokinesis [or PK] in 1934. Since some professional gamblers have long alleged that they can make the dice or the little white roulette ball "obey" their desires, Dr. Rhine initiated his testing for PK with dice-throwing experiments and openly sought volunteers who claimed to have used "mind over matter" to bring in tangible rewards at the gaming tables. In his *The Reach of the Mind* (1947), Dr. Rhine set forth an analysis of his data and concluded that psychokinesis had been established beyond all question. Although some researchers might separate such "psi" attributes as telepathy and clairvoyance from psychokinesis on the grounds that the former are sensory phenomena while the latter is a motor phenomena (mind affecting matter), Dr. Rhine insists that the existence of one implies the existence of the other, and that they are closely related.

Dice-throwers with marked control over the dice were much more successful at the beginning of a run. The same sort of "decline" effect that has been noted so often by agents evaluating telepathic subjects in card-guessing experiments appears to be strongly in evidence in testing for PK.

The Duke University parapsychology laboratories observed other similarities between the PK facet of "psi" abilities and the other "extrasensory" phenomena. For example, mechanical devices made no differences in the effectiveness of PK. Neither did distance. Once again, as in testing for telepathy or clairvoyance, a relaxed, informal atmosphere produced the best psychokinetic results. Another important similarity between the two types of paranormal abilities is that the person who expects success and truly believes in his ability to produce the desired result will always score much higher than the individual who is indifferent to "psi" manifestations.

It was through Dr. Rhine, then, that Hurley met Olof Jonsson. The respected parapsychologist had suggested that Jonsson would prove of eminent value in the execution of Hurley's project. The professor found Jonsson to be " . . .a perfect example of the Wordsworthian ideal of one wholly in tune with nature and in rapport with all. He is a complete man, endowed with a gift which imposes heavy responsibilities on him—and is the source of frequent troubles."

One night in the summer of 1964, Hurley had been visiting Jonsson in his home where they had been discussing ESP and working experiments. Even the spiritual man must eat, and they decided to take a break in their work and visit a neighborhood restaurant. After finishing dessert, Jonsson asked Hurley if he would like to see him move an object in the dining room.

"I dumbly nodded my head," Hurley wrote in the August 22, 1965, issue of the *Chicago Tribune Magazine*. "Jonsson gazed at the ceiling, from which hung numerous chandeliers. Each fixture was composed of three lights capable of independent movement. That is to say, if you were to touch one globe, the other two would not move."

Hurley pointed to a fixture across the room, specifying that he wanted Olof to move the globe nearest the wall.

"I had full view of it," Hurley states. "Jonsson said it was beginning to move. I, who had been staring intently at the metal sphere, said I could not be sure. Olof suggested I take a closer look. I found the globe in motion. I asked Olof to make it stop—and it did. I requested the sensitive to make it move again. His reply was a more dramatic movement of the sphere."

Hurley ran his hand around the fixture to check for drafts. He found none, and he noted that the other two globes were perfectly still.

A waitress stood near their table, tossing clean silverware into compartments on a serving table. Hurley asked her if she could see anything unusual about the globes in the light fixture.

"She glanced perfunctorily at the ceiling and matter-of-factly answered that one of the globes was moving," Hurley writes.

Two things were brought home to the investigator at that moment: "I was not mesmerized, and a psychic phenomenon could stare a person directly in the face and he wouldn't necessarily be aware of it. I am sure this has happened more than once to many of us."

Two Swedish doctors, Anders Perntz and Sven Erik Larsson, made the following report on several psychokinetic experiments which they conducted with Olof Jonsson under full control:

"One of the controllers placed a pewter candlestick weighing 1.25 kilograms on the table while Jonsson stood two or three yards away. The controller ordered that Jonsson extend his hand toward the candlestick. Jonsson had not touched the candlestick beforehand. A controller had fetched it from a shelf and immediately set it upon the table. Before the eyes of all, the candlestick turned 180 degrees on the table.

"Another telekinetic experiment was performed with a piece of wood sculpture which weighed 50 grams. Olof Jonsson stood in front of the table and the object slid at an even speed across the table top and fell down to the floor."

Jonsson lived for a short time in the home of Dr. W. of

Stockholm, Sweden. "Telekinetic phenomena took place daily," Dr. W. later stated, "and sometimes they were completely spontaneous. After Olof Jonsson left, the phenomena continued for several days. Pictures slipped askew, objects fell to the floor. . . ."

The late Danish psychical researcher and photographer Sven Turck conducted repeated tests of Jonsson's telekinetic powers. "Olof Jonsson possesses not only unusual telepathic powers, but he has also an especially great power of telekinesis," Turck once told Swedish journalist Stig Arne Kjellen. "Every trick has been guarded against in our tests by the strong controls which exist in my photographic laboratory. I prophesy for him a brilliant future in the service of science."

In Turck's laboratory in Copenhagen, the photographer invited numerous scientists to test the mediumistic prowess of several sensitives, including Jonsson. "I subjected most of our mediums here in Copenhagen to a critical investigation and afterward organized a little group of ten members of the highest capacities," Turck once wrote, defining his investigative procedure. "We got together twice weekly at my laboratory at Vesterbro where we spent our evenings around a large worktable. We sang happy songs, which had no religious character such as those generally associated with seances in Spiritualistic circles.

"Our intent was to make a completely technical attempt to bring about telekinesis and levitation—two groups of phenomena which are especially well-suited to photographing. I set up three cameras at different angles, so that one always showed the action from behind, one from underneath, and one from above. Twenty times we had set this up before things began to happen."

Turck's experiments took place in very subdued light and both people and pieces of furniture were equipped with phosphorescent bands. During an early session, a zither that Turck kept in the room began to emit sounds as if the strings were being plucked by unseen hands. When Turck placed the instrument in its case, the phenomenon continued without interruption.

Chairs and objects began to move. The large worktable rose up on one leg and began to whirl around its own base, pirouetting faster and faster. Turck's greatest wish was that they might get the table to soar freely in the air so that he might photograph the phenomenon of levitation. A few evenings later, the photographer was able to capture the fulfillment of his wish on the film of three cameras.

As the twice-weekly sessions progressed, the phenomena began to gain strength. The worktable floated through the big doors out into Turck's studio, moving well ahead of the seance's participants. Once it entered the studio it danced about the 15 x 30-foot floor.

"One after another we sat down upon the table, while it moved at a good rate from one end of the room to the other," Turck reported. "At one time, six people found themselves on the lively, wandering piece of furniture at the same time.

"Later it lifted itself up and passed above our heads. Once it had achieved this elevation, none of the participants came closer than two yards to the table."

These phenomena were repeated often during the course of several months' of sittings in Sven Turck's laboratory and were always dutifully recorded by the trio of cameras which had been loaded with infrared film. On one occasion, a large commode, of such a weight that two men could not lift it without great effort, was moved soundlessly out into the middle of the laboratory floor.

After a year of sittings in the twice-weekly laboratory-controlled seances, the group achieved the levitation of a human being. Medium Borge Michaelson was lifted from his seat and raised up to the ceiling.

"He circled around up there above the table and then fell to the knees of Madame Melloni, softly, without the least bump," Turck later recorded. "Madame Melloni scarcely felt the force of his fall. The three cameras had flashed and presented us with proof that we had not been victims of hallucination. I succeeded in photographing five such air rides."

Stig Arne Kjellen says that Sven Turck had never been able to believe in such dramatic displays of psychokinetic force until he had become a participant in the sessions held in his own laboratory. "Sven Turck was a robust, healthy, and positive man, without the slightest trace of fanaticism or tendency to fantasize," Kjellen has commented.

In principle, the psychokinetic moving of a candlestick is just as remarkable as the moving of a heavy table. Both feats are quite impossible in the view of orthodox science. The series of photographs taken during Turck's experiments in Copenhagen were carefully examined by five of Denmark's foremost photographic technicians, among them the director of the Danish photographic professional school, Theodore Andresen, who had full access to the photographic negatives. Each of the photographers agreed that no manipulations whatsoever had been worked upon the negatives.

Professor Preben Plum wrote of Turck's experiments:

"In 1946 and 1947 I was present at about twenty research evenings at Sven Turck's house, Vestsbrogade 37, Copenhagen. These research sessions utilized the mediums Borge Michaelson, Mrs. Vestfjord, Mrs. Melloni, and the Swedish engineer, Jonsson. It is my conclusion that those experiments I have witnessed at Sven Turck's must be described as systematic research work in the realm of parapsychology. Turck is an orderly and patient experimenter who, with uncommon energy and unquestioned experience, has progressed in making special areas of research in parapsychology the ground for further investigation. He has a particular wish to control and test telekinetic phenomena."

Professor Torben Laurent of the Royal Technical High School has reported an experiment with Olof Jonsson during which the sensitive employed both clairvoyance and psychokinesis:

"Engineer Jonsson had no occasion to introduce hidden technical aids into my office. Those present were members of my family, as well as some of my assistants and members of their families.

"Jonsson asked me to shuffle my own deck of cards, spread it out on my desk, picture side down, draw out a random card without looking at it, put it into an envelope (such were found in the drawer of my desk), seal it, and lay the envelope on the desk. Meanwhile, he himself had left the room so that I, unhampered, could see to it that there was no mischief afoot with the cards.

"When the job was finished, Jonsson was called in; and he

asked if he might borrow one of my dice. I gave him one, and he threw it on the envelope. It turned up a five.

"Jonsson then said: 'The card is a five of hearts—please look at it.'

"He turned out to be correct. The card was a five of hearts.

"The card and the dice were photographed and after the film was developed we could all establish that we had not been victims of 'suggestion.' That day the test was done twice more with the same success. Olof Jonsson insisted that he knew what card I had selected, through clairvoyance, and that he had influenced the dice with telekinesis."

Stig Arne Kjellen, who became a meticulous scholar in the realm of the paranormal, has observed that psychokinetic phenomena presuppose a "medium" around whom remarkable transferences take place. Accepting the reality of psychokinesis, the spontaneous phenomena which have been reported in association with accounts and legends of sorcery may in some instances have a factual background. However, unless the phenomena can be produced in a laboratory under controlled conditions which the investigator himself provides, psycho-kinesis remains aloof from scientific examination and excluded from orthodox acceptance.

"As the telekinetic power is very rare and its production under laboratory investigations is still rarer, the appearance of a 'medium,' who, on the experiment-leader's command, in full light and under all thinkable controls, shows a telekinetic phenomenon, is something of a wishful dream," commented Kjellen. "However, such a person does exist. I refer to the engineer, Olof Jonsson."

Kjellen has termed Jonsson "the strong man of the super-natural." Although the accolade was well-intentioned, Olof would object strenuously to Kjellen's use of the word "super-natural." To Jonsson's own way of thinking, all the remarkable abilities which he has demonstrated since early childhood lie latent in everyone.

Kjellen recorded 140 carefully controlled experiments in telekinesis before Jonsson left Sweden in 1953 at the invitation of Professor J. B. Rhine, who asked him to come to Duke

University for a series of parapsychological tests. The writer-researcher Kjellen stated that the spontaneous telekinetic phenomena, which he witnessed in addition to the controlled experiments, would "...certainly reach to double that number." Moreover, in the informally conducted demonstrations, Kjellen insists that he executed "all thinkable precautionary steps under the most diverse conditions."

According to Kjellen:

"Olof Jonsson's power in the telekinetic realm shows a vitality and a strength which is nowhere described in the international parapsychological literature. Under the conditions which I myself could set up, he had the utmost exeptional power, that could on direct command suddenly produce these phenomena.

"Without any previous preparations whatsoever, accompanied by people he had never met before and in places so distracting and un-occult as restaurants and hotel vestibules, he got bottles, flowers, jars, ashtrays, toothpick holders, and candlesticks into motion, while talking with an altogether untroubled smile.

"Frequently these demonstrations took place with Jonsson situated a great distance away, and yet he was able to exert such force that, on some occasions, objects were moved several yards in one direction or another, sometimes directly up into the air. . . .

"From a distance of several yards and sometimes without even being present in the room, Jonsson put various phenomena into action. A few moments of concentration, wherein he was in no obvious way separated from the 'everyday things of life,' was all that was necessary by way of preparation."

Olof Jonsson's comments on producing psychokinetic phenomena:

I must feel in the mood for telekinesis; that is a most necessary condition. Things must feel right—it is as simple as that. If a dozen so-called controllers with sarcastic sneers search me in an effort to discover strands of hair, strings, collapsible bamboo canes and all that they think is needed to produce such phenomena, then things do not obviously feel "right."

Have you ever seen a champion diver perform a good high jump if he was being hissed and laughed to scorn? But when I feel happy, then I know the trial will succeed. Enthusiasm can be infectious for me, and I have many times had the experience that the power to produce telekinetic phenomena becomes markedly stronger when people around me are happy and believe in me. Serenity or matter-of-fact objectivity also provide excellent backgrounds for the production of telekinetic phenomena.

When I am in the proper mood, I can experiment for several hours without becoming tired. As you know, it often happens that the phenomena grow in strength. I must feel confident that I will succeed. That is why I have often led into telekinesis with little telepathic experimentation. Suddenly I feel I can do it!

Someone places a heavy book on a table. I begin to concentrate, and with a completely usual process of thought, together with a hand gesture in the direction of the object, I get the book to leave the table. I cannot say that I have ever thought this to be so remarkable. But, indeed, it has been a pleasure to irritate one or another professional magician who cannot accept the fact that I am able to accomplish such manifestations without cheating or without employing mechanical aids or confederates.

On what would now be thousands of occasions, I have had experimenters set a bottle on a table. While I stood several yards away, I have made the bottle fall heavily to the floor. Many investigators have sought to find some trick that I employ which can give the evidence of telekinesis an "acceptable" explanation, but at that task they have all been nonplussed. My demonstrations have nothing to do with any sort of trickery. My telekinesis is simply a matter of a certain power which somehow flows out of me and gets an object to vibrate so much that it begins to move. Now and then I have cracked glass with this power.

On one occasion in an entertainment hall, I staked a coin on a wheel with fifty-two cards. I chose the queen of hearts, and told my companions that I would win. The roulette wheel seemed to make a double stop exactly at the queen of hearts, and I was able to cash in on the winnings. Through mental radiation I got the roulette wheel to rotate more slowly. I could have broken the bank if I had wanted to, but such tactics violate my principles.

One time I satisfied myself by winning ten chocolate cakes in succession on another wheel. Before the eyes of the astonished concession operator, I freely gave out the cakes to some little girls, as thankful as they were hopeful, who had stood around me in a circle looking on.

Olof Jonsson constantly mentions the fact that "conditions" must be right before he can achieve psychokinetic effects. Every psychical, psychological, and physical factor must have been exactly right on that night in June, 1969, when Olof accomplished one of the most impressive psychokinetic demonstrations with which I am familiar. The Ursitti family of Dolton, Illinois, together with a guest and—eventually—a good portion of the suburb, witnessed the experiment:

Arlene Ursitti: Let's see, there was my mother, Dorothy Ursitti, Kelly Britt—she's an actress who's in *Promises, Promises* in Chicago now—and Betty and Olof. It was just a fast get-together. I wanted Kelly to meet Olof.

Well, first of all that night, I saw colors around people, just as clear as if you'd be watching television. Olof was sitting across from Kelly, and it started out like it was the flame of the candle, kind of teardrop shaped. It started out on each of their foreheads and it would go right up into the light. As it would go up, it would change colors. The colors were real bright, but each was different, and they would go directly up into the light. I'd never had anything like that happen to me. These colors were so pretty that I was screaming. I thought everyone in the room could see them, but no one else could.

"What was she seeing, Olof?"

Olof Jonsson: The energy that I was sending out at that time. Many people have seen this and told me about it.

"You were sending a thought to this girl?"

Jonsson: Yes.

"How did Arlene happen to tune into this when she had never seen anything like it before?"

Jonsson: She was in that circle, so she somehow absorbed it. She just happened to be tuned in for that experiment.

"Go on, Arlene, about the *really* big experiment."

Miss Ursitti: Yes, well, Mother said that the lights were too bright. She wanted Olof to do some more experiments, but she thought the light was too bright.

Jonsson: *Ja*, she said something like "the light is too strong." Of course I wanted to do something about it, so I meditated. I concentrated that the light was going to become dimmer, and it did.

Miss Ursitti: You told us all to raise our hands toward the light, then as we lowered our hands, the light became dimmer. We thought at first that it was just the one light in that room that he had dimmed, but when we checked, we found that he had dimmed every light in the house. Then my mother got worried about what the neighbors would think because our house lights were dimmed and all the neighbors' lights were bright. So Olof said, "Well, we'll dim the neighbors' lights, too." And he did.

"But when you first looked outside, all your neighbors' lights were bright. Only your house was dim."

Miss Ursitti: Yes, one of the neighbors even has a spotlight in front of his house, and that was just as bright as could be until Olof dimmed it.

"How did the neighbors react?"

Miss Ursitti: They all came out of their houses and looked up and down the street. They were milling around and talking to each other and wondering what had happened to dim their lights. Olof even told us how long the lights would be dim. I think it was twenty-five minutes.

Jonsson: Twenty-five and one half minutes.

Miss Ursitti: Mother went outside and she could see that the lights were dim on our side of the street as far as she could see. The lights on the other side of the street were as bright as ever. One of the neighbors called the power plant, but they told him there was nothing wrong that they could determine.

"How far did this area of dimmed lights extend?"

Miss Ursitti: I have a cousin who lives on this one street in Dolton, and right across from them is a liquor store. She said that the lights in the liquor store were dimmed, but the houses on her side of the street stayed bright

Another cousin lives in Riverdale, that's the next suburb, and her husband, who has always been a non-believer in ESP and the whole works, said that he didn't know what was going on, but the lights were so dim that his son couldn't see to do his homework.

"So it seemed to cover one side of the street all the way from your house through Dolton and on into Riverdale?"

Miss Ursitti: Yes. The next day all the schoolchildren were talking about the strange dimout. A friend who rides the commuter train said that the dimout was the main topic of conversation. She overheard two men cursing the power company because one of them had called the company and was told that there was no shortage or any trouble at all.

"Olof, what did you do to make this happen?"

Jonsson: I know that I can do the same thing to a car motor. I concentrate and lift my hand like this and there seems to be some kind of chain reaction. That was why so many lights were dimmed in Dolton.

That night I meditated on the light and some kind of power went out from me. I don't know how it happens, but I did this a few times in Sweden, too, and no one could explain it. Somehow the energy from my brain or something within me sets up a kind of chain reaction that interferes with electro-magnetic generators.

Chapter Sixteen

GHOSTS, HAUNTINGS, AND THE PHENOMENA
OF THE SEANCE ROOM

By the time that the haunted family in Varnersborg contacted Olof Jonsson, they had been visited by the eerie manifestations for fourteen nights in succession. The phenomena seemed to center around the large table where they ate their evening meals. Knocks would thud so heavily on its surface that eating utensils and tableware would be sent flying to the floor. Then, after the violent knockings, a flickering blob of light would materialize in a corner of the dining room.

"We've thought of appealing to Pastor Lund," the head of the family, Oscar Petersen, told Olof, "but we know that the Lutheran church is not especially receptive to tales of ghosts and requests for exorcism. Berit, my wife, has suggested that we contact Father Larsen, but. . ."

"Why not let me see what I am able to accomplish before you consult the clergy," Olof interrupted. "Sometimes if the entity is particularly malignant, prayers, incense, and holy water only serve to irritate it and bring about even more violent displays. Then, too, it seems that religious denominations and dogmas have little meaning on the other side of the veil."

Petersen agreed to suffer one more night of the phenomena until Olof could visit his home on the following evening.

"I hated to leave the man and his family to face the

Unknown another night, but it was impossible for me to cancel plans and attend to them at once," Olof recalled recently. "Although I am continually being called a medium, I am not really a Spiritualist in the full sense of the term. I have no spirit guides, and while I accept the possibility of entities contacting us from beyond the grave, I really believe that the phenomenon which we call a 'ghost' is most often a sort of radiation of the human personality which retains the memories of the physically deceased person.

"I also believe that many times that which is contacted at seances is actually this radiation rather than the actual surviving entity. It is my opinion that, in most instances, the actual Soul of a person has gone on to different spiritual realm, or dimension, and the 'ghost' is but an astral form left behind."

When Olof arrived at the Petersen residence, he made certain to time his appearance so that he might witness the full event of the manifestation. "Go on about your meal and your usual routine, as if I were not here," Olof told the Petersens. "Let me observe just what it is that visits you."

The family did as they were told and sat down around the large and heavy table to begin their evening meal.

The first knock was so violent that it sent a metal platter of fish to the floor, scattering its contents across the carpet. The second thud sounded next to Mrs. Petersen's plate and caused her to jerk back in reflex action. Olof stood calmly off to one side of the table, indicating by a gesture of his upraised hand that the family should remain seated

"There are usually three heavy knocks before the minor rappings begin," Petersen told the psychic.

The words were scarcely out of his mouth when a pitcher of water shattered and drenched a bowl of hot vegetables and the three Petersen children. The youngest child began to cry, and Mrs. Petersen left her chair to comfort him. As she did so, her chair was tipped over and the floor sounded with heavy footsteps which seemed to withdraw to a corner of the room.

"And now comes the light," Petersen sighed. "The phenomenon will have run its course."

"Not tonight," Olof corrected him, as he watched the flickering globe of light materialize in the corner opposite the one in which he had positioned himself. "I shall concentrate on sending psychic energy to the light so that we might better see what it is that is molesting you."

With Olof directing his mental energy toward the pulsating globule of light, the nebulous pocket of radiation began to take on form.

"My God, Berit," Petersen shouted at his wife, "get the children out of here!"

The mother gathered her children under her arms and ushered them quickly out of the dining room. The light had begun to take on the shape of an elderly woman whose face was an ugly mask of hatred. The image was not an appropriate one for small children to carry with them to their beds.

"It. . .it appears to be Sigrid," Petersen said. "But why. . .?"

Olof had slipped into a light trance. "She is angry, very angry that you have the table," Olof told the man. "And she says that you have cheated her and lied to her."

Petersen slumped into a chair. He had become very pale. He opened his mouth, made a few inarticulate sounds, then seemed to think better of it, and chose to remain silent.

"She says that you have stolen from her daughter, that you have. . ."

"But can this really be Sigrid's ghost returned from beyond the grave?" Petersen wanted to know. "Surely she would know that these things are not so."

As Olof returned to a level of mind more attuned to the material plane, the image of the old woman began to lose its definition and became an abstract arrangement of flickering lights. "This would seem to be a memory pattern of hatred that has been directed at you by someone in the last moments before death," the psychic explained. "It is of such strength that it can produce those telekinetic effects on your table."

"It. . .it isn't really a ghost, then?" Petersen asked, still confused.

"It *is* a ghost," Olof clarified, "but it is not really this Sigrid to whom you refer. What we saw was her astral form, which had been set free with a residue of her memories and her emotions. This astral form is acting very much like a puppet, only it is doing the bidding of a puppeteer who is no longer living."

"Sigrid was an older friend of my mother's," Petersen offered. "She was like an aunt to me, even though we were not really related. Sigrid had married late in life, and then her husband died and left her with an infant daughter. The daughter and I were childhood playmates, and it was Sigrid's hope that we would marry. Neither the young lady nor I felt romantically inclined toward one another, but we remained good friends."

Petersen paused to light his pipe, then once he had the tobacco burning, he set the pipe in an ashtray, as if the smoke nauseated him. "Could it be that Sigrid was still alive that day and misunderstood our conversation?" he asked the empty space before him. "I became Sigrid's attorney as soon as I had my law degree," Petersen said, turning to face Olof. "She was always a headstrong woman, and in her later years she became mentally confused, suspicious of everyone to the point of paranoia. On her deathbed, she charged me once again with my responsibilities as her executor, and she made a special point of reminding me that her daughter was to receive certain items of personal property, such as this magnificent old table here."

Petersen picked up the pipe and another match, then decided better of it and resumed speaking: "Sigrid went faster than anticipated toward the end, and her daughter was unable to get to her bedside before she lapsed into a final coma. The doctor said something to me about what a grand old woman Sigrid had been, and I agreed, stating that at least I would have the old table and certain antiques by which to remember her.

"You see," Petersen hastened to add before Olof could think the worst, "Sigrid's daughter and I had had an earlier conversation in which she stated that she did not want the expense of hauling the heavy pieces of furniture to her home in Stockholm. She told me that she did not really care about antiques anyway, and since I had always admired the pieces, I should keep them for myself as a remembrance of her mother. I protested, then consented if she would allow me to deduct a certain sum from my legal fees in return. Now it appears that Sigrid must have somehow been able to hear me utter those words to the doctor, and she has cursed me for a thief!"

Olof assured the man that there was no need to become upset. "The kind of ghost that is troubling you is very much like a persistent messenger boy who will not put off from delivering the message that has been entrusted to him," he explained. "Just as the ghost was formed by the dying brain of a human being, so can it be dissipated by a living brain."

Olof meditated for a few moments, then entered another level of consciousness which permitted him to direct psychic energy toward the flickering lights in the corner. Within seconds, the "ghost" had disappeared.

"That was not just the ordinary brain of an ordinary human being that accomplished that feat," Petersen remarked in awe at Jonsson's psychic prowess.

Olof shrugged and smiled. "But remember, I did not destroy the *soul* of Sigrid, I merely dispersed the telepathic-telekinetic energy which she directed toward you in her last moments of confused hatred. Your 'ghost' has been exorcised."

After listening to Olof Jonsson recount this story, it occurred to me to ask why so much of the phenomena of the seance room seems to center around a tilting table, a rapping table, or a floating table. Olof replied with an interesting digression on what he termed the "table dance":

The table dance has an ancient history. Through the ages people in Scandinavia have used this phenomenon for amusement and possible edification on dark, winter nights. For the most part, they have entertained themselves by posing questions that are answered with knocks, or a leg-jerk for yes or no. Occasionally the answers have been optimistic and positive; other times they have been extremely misleading and uninformative. In many instances the "answer" has depended upon the skillfulness of the inquirers and their ability to interpret the response of the table.

If strong powers have been at work among those seated around the table, the table can manage to behave like a ghost and glide across the floor, occasionally even standing on its end and pounding the floor so violently that neighbors grow uneasy. It is not unheard of that table legs have been broken off and damage has been done to other furniture in the room.

It is a very common misconception that it is necessary to use a round table without nails or screws in order for the phenomenon of table dancing to be effective. I have been present when heavy oak tables, yards long, have shown a capacity to move which one would not believe of such massive pieces of furniture.

Skeptical persons who attend table dances for the first time like to accuse one or more participants seated around the table of having purposely brought on the movement with their hands or feet. If the phenomenon has not been deliberately faked, however hard the skeptics try they will not find any fraud in the table dance. On the contrary, soon they will realize that there are other powers at work which no one can consciously develop.

Now and then, if the conditions are suitable, the table dance may set in motion other phenomena in the room. Pictures may slip from their hooks; vases may crash to the floor; and a great many other things may happen. Yes, now and then it has happened that someone in the group has felt movements as of hands on their faces and breasts. Puffs of wind, like waves of intense cold moving through the room, are not rare; noise and light can also reveal themselves.

Photographer and psychical researcher Sven Turck described many particularly conspicuous manifestations which occurred at seances in his studio on Vesterbo Street in Copenhagen. Big, heavy tables lifted themselves to the ceiling, in spite of several persons "on board" as passengers.

One medium who sat in our group at Sven Turck's was named Michelson. He was able to bring about veritable flights up to the ceiling, and on some occasions his clothes were torn from his body without anyone's comprehending how such actions could come about. During a number of seances, a long, thick rope would wind itself repeatedly around Michelson, as if it were a boa constrictor. Michelson grew to become deathly frightened by this rope, which he thought meant to strangle him.

During one seance, Turck's dog found its way into the laboratory. The animal jumped up exactly as if it saw something in front of it, barked angrily, then looked horribly frightened and crept away with its tail between its legs.

Such phenomena eventually got on the nerves of the mediums as well as the participants in these particularly dramatic seances—especially when the phenomena continued in Turck's private dwelling and in the homes of us mediums. At last it got to the point where the photographer and his family had to abandon their place and settle in the country. From Sven Turck's experience, the psychical researcher should realize that he must be cautions in his traffic with the "powers" that lie behind the phenomena of the seance room.

What are these powers? It is not enough to speak of the role of the subconscious or the unconscious muscular movements of the participants in such instances of widespread phenomena. The camera, film, and flash attachment can register the very moment when the psychically influenced objects began to move. But the origin of the power itself lies far beyond the photographer's lens.

Danish author-researcher Poul Thorsen witnessed a number of psychokinetic seance room demonstrations accomplished with Olof Jonsson acting as the medium. In Thorsen's opinion: "Engineer Jonsson's telekinetic demonstrations are always brought about through a conscious, concentrated effort of willpower, and are totally free of the cooperation of spirit guides and the like. When certain objects, as for example a flask standing on a table, moves as a result of. . .a concentration of will. . .we are facing a common telekinetic phenomenon. We are also facing a telekinetic phenomenon when a slip of paper, which I, myself, had inserted in the neck of a milk bottle, flies out of the bottle with a noise. . . .When clairvoyance is also added to telekinesis, we have an interesting combination of psychic and physical phenomena. . . ."

In his book, *Man's Unknown Powers*, Thorsen describes a seance during which he and five other people, none of whom had ever before met Jonsson, were present.

Among many other phenomena that evening I shall mention one, when someone present—and this was repeated several times—took a card out of the deck without anyone's looking at the card. After that we all sat down around a circular table, which on the medium's command should give the color and value of the card through knockings. In some instances the medium sat with the others beside the table; in others, he stood behind them.

Each time the table knocked with very powerful blows the correct value of the card, and one time so violently that the leg of the table went to pieces.

All these experiments, therefore, showed a combination of telekinesis and clairvoyance. This medium showed, as he himself said, "by means of his subconscious," which one of all the unknown cards it was, and through an act of mental power, he raised the table to knock out the value of the card. The medium accomplished everything without the pre-engaged assistance of any invisible beings.

Nor was I aware of any "invisible beings" at the seance that I attended in the home of a Chicago-area schoolteacher in which Ruth Zimmerman and Olof Jonsson served as the mediums. But the table did become quite lively and unfortunately, dealt the soft-spoken and gentle Mrs. Zimmerman a severe blow in the abdomen, as it rocked violently on its side. The low blow seemed to end the table dance for that night, but Mrs. Zimmerman did attract a number of glowing, firefly-sized lights around her face, and there were a few raps on the table's surface.

Ruth Zimmerman is one of Olof Jonsson's favorite "batteries." That is to say, the two mediums are *harmonious*, to use Olof's pet term, and they work well together. Ruth is a medium of no small ability herself, but she is one of those rare individuals who can subordinate her ego to another's during a seance and genuinely cooperate to produce a fruitful session. Modestly, Ruth maintains that her own abilities are still in the development stage, and she insists that she is contented to work in the shadow of a master such as Olof Jonsson.

"Ruth is very good," Olof says of his friend. "She gives excellent readings and has produced ectoplasm and a wide variety of manifestations during seances. One day I know that she will become very famous as a medium."

Ingrid Bergstrom: You want to hear about seances? I will tell you about a seance no one will believe. Betty attended it just before she married Olof, and she became so frightened that afterward I asked her if she would still go through with the wedding.

Betty Jonsson: I was so frightened that I was actually crying.

"Well, tell me about it. Where was it held?"

Mrs. Bergstrom: It was held at Verdandi's, in our spooky room. That's where they used to have the slot machines in the days when the clubs could have gambling. And there's still quite an atmosphere in there, I tell you. We used it as a storeroom for tables and silverware and things we weren't using.

Well, anyway, we had the lights dimmed, but not completely off. Betty held Olof's right hand and I held his left hand, and we had our feet on his feet so that he could not move. I think we sat for half an hour before something happened.

Mrs. Jonsson: You were singing a little bit, remember?

Mrs. Bergstrom: Yes, and then we heard footsteps, like dancing. Like someone dancing a waltz. Then the steps came from all over. A cloth came off a table without disturbing a tray of glasses sitting on it and came whisking by my face. I had an awful, cold feeling.

Mrs. Jonsson: Then a glass came flying through the air.

Mrs. Bergstrom: And for anybody to have reached those glasses, he would have had to go stepping over stacked-up chairs and tables. But that glass just came floating off a tray.

Mrs. Jonsson: Brad, you could hear things flying through the room; you could hear footsteps running around. I had always enjoyed attending seances, but this was the first time that I had ever been afraid. I mean, I had one of Olof's arms, and Ingrid had the other, and we both covered his feet with our own, and since we were the only three people in the room, who was throwing things all over the place?

Mrs. Bergstrom: The heavy table at which we were sitting came up, and another table that was sitting on top of another across the room just came up by itself and crashed to the floor.

Mrs. Jonsson: Ingrid, tell Brad about the seance we held at your place last Valentine's Day.

Mrs. Bergstrom: *Ja*, my cousin from Detroit and her husband wanted to meet Betty and Olof. My cousin's husband had made up his mind that he was not going to believe anything that happened that night, and he still says that if he had not seen those things with his own eyes, he never would have believed it. Now, he says, he sits at his job and wonders about the meaning of it all.

We had dinner and afterward we placed our hands on the dining room table. It is made of teak and it is very big. It weighs, perhaps, over two hundred pounds. But all of a sudden it began to rise and bang itself to the floor. After a while the young couple, who were having a party below us, knocked on the door and asked if I were trying to tell them that they were disturbing us. Oh, no, I told them, it is just my table. Olof Jonsson is here and we are making the table walk by itself.

Now, Betty, I am not going to send you a bill, but one of the table legs is broken. Who would have thought such a heavy wood could shatter? But it raised itself so high and slammed itself down so hard so many times, just as if it were angry.

I remember once moving out of its way, because it was coming after me. And it nearly got my cousin's husband into a corner. He, too, wondered if it were mad at him.

"How were you placed at the table? Were you standing or sitting? Did you have your hands on the table?"

Mrs. Bergstrom: We sat at first with our hands lightly touching the table. When it started to move, I looked to see if anybody was trying to move it with their hands, but then everybody had their hands above the table.

"Where was Olof?"

Mrs. Bergstrom: He was standing away from the table. He had been sitting for just a little while at the very beginning of the seance, but he soon rose to stand in a corner of the room.

When the table began to jump, everyone moved away. That heavy table jumped like a horse. Everybody backed away from it. It was like a living thing.

If we have demonstrated any one thing in this book, it is to be hoped that we have shown that Olof Jonsson does not require any special trappings or environment for the exercise of his incredible talents. A booth in a restaurant is as compatible to Jonsson's abilities as is a darkened seance room with a circle of sitters.

Soon after Britta Seaberg met Olof Jonsson in 1954, she and Gunnar, her husband-to-be, sat visiting with the newly-immigrated psychic in the Swedish Engineers' Club in Chicago.

"Olof asked me to write something on a piece of paper while

he went to a corner of the room to meditate," Mrs. Seaberg recalled for this author recently. "I was new to psychics and ESP experiments, so I simply wrote, 'I don't know what to write' with a pencil and crumpled the paper to hold between my palms. Olof was far away from our table and could not see what I had written.

"So Olof came back to the table and asked Gunnar and another friend, who were sitting across from me, if they would concentrate on what I had written. When he came back to the table again, he handed me a piece of paper. On it he had written the same words as I had *in exactly my own handwriting.* It was as if he had made a photocopy of my own piece of paper. I do not believe a handwriting expert could tell the two apart. And his copy even had an impression of the wood grain of the table-top, just as my own sheet did!"

Ingrid and Gustav Bergstrom first met Olof at the *Svenska Gillet,* the Swedish Friendship Club. On their first meeting, although Olof impressed them with his abilities, the Bergstroms concluded that the engineer had simply made some lucky guesses.

"But it was, I believe, in 1955 that we had that dinner party at our home when Olle said that he would lift a bottle into the air and set it down on the floor by using only his thoughts," Ingrid told me. "I guess nobody there believed that he could do it, and Gustav never would have believed it if he hadn't seen it. But Olle took a lilac out of a vase and said, 'I take the life out of this lilac and put it into the bottle.'

"Then Olle went out in the hallway. He could not even see us or the bottle, and we were all holding hands around the table, watching the bottle for the slightest sign of movement.

"Then all of a sudden that bottle went up into the air and right down to the floor. It did not roll to the edge and fall off, mind you. It went straight up, then over, then down to the floor.

"When Olle came back into the room, he gave me back the lilac and told me to put it back with the other flowers. 'By tomorrow,' he said, 'it will be brown.' And, hand on my heart, it was brown, though all the others were healthy."

How does it feel to meet someone like Olof Jonsson and come to know him well?

"Well, I have accepted the idea that Olle is a little bit more than the rest of us," Gunnar Seaberg said. "He has something that maybe the rest of us don't use the way we should, or could, but the last few years a lot of people have begun to accept things that they never did before."

"Soon after we met," Britta Seaberg told me, "Olle found a lost object for a girl friend of mine, then he began to tell her things about her past life that absolutely no one knew. She threw up her hands and said that she wanted nothing to do with such a wizard.

"I did not feel that Olof was doing anything anti-religious," Britta went on, "but it was rather spooky the way he could know those things about Mildred. When you find out the things he has said are true, you almost do feel as though he has true supernatural powers. But after I have learned to know him, he has told me that we all have these abilities within us."

Perhaps Danish author Poul Thorsen said it best when he wrote: "Olof Jonsson is one of the few mediums who can get us to recognize the possibility that hidden powers deserving of serious study lie within each of us."

Chapter Seventeen

TELEPORTING OBJECTS

Mrs. Dolly Mitchell of Lansing, Illinois, told me that she and her family had witnessed many unusual demonstrations by Olof, but she considered one experiment particularly memorable.

"This feat was performed with our son, Tommy, then twelve years old, in the company of about ten relatives and friends," Mrs. Mitchell said. "Olof told Tommy to think of a card—I don't remember which one he chose, but for convenience I shall say the ace of hearts. He then told Tommy to cut a deck of cards into four piles—I must point out here that this was my deck of cards and Olof never touched them.

"Olof pointed to the first pile of cards and asked Tommy if he wanted the ace of hearts to be in that pile. Tommy said, 'No.' We immediately picked up the pile and looked through it. The ace of hearts was not there," Mrs. Mitchell said.

"Olof asked Tommy the same question with the other three piles," Mrs. Mitchell went on," and Tommy answered 'no' each time. And each time the rest of us looked through the pile, but there was no ace of hearts.

"After Tommy had said 'no' for all four piles, my brother-in-law picked up all the cards and examined them again. There was *no* ace of hearts.

"Olof then asked Tommy to shuffle the cards and repeat the

performance; that is, cut the deck into four separate piles," Mrs. Mitchell remembered. "Again he asked Tom if he wanted the ace of hearts to be in the first pile. Tom said 'no' and we looked through the pile to determine that the card was not there. He did the same thing with the next two piles, but no ace of hearts. Finally, when Olof pointed to the fourth pile, Tommy said he wanted the ace of hearts to be in that pile.

"Olof told Tommy to put the cards behind his back and to take them out one at a time, in any order he pleased, but no matter how he took them out, the ace of hearts would be the last card he chose. In all honesty, the ace of hearts was the third to the last card, but we considered the performance completely amazing."

The mechanics of the above experiment have been described earlier, in this book, and I have witnessed similar demonstrations on several occasions. The "amazing" element in the experiment is that Olof apparently makes a card disappear without at any time touching or manipulating the deck. For the professional magician who says that he can duplicate the experiment, I remind him of these limiting conditions: 1) the use of a deck never before opened or touched by the performer; 2) at no time may the performer manipulate the deck or come within several feet of the deck; 3) the card is chosen mentally and at random and the deck never leaves the possession of the witnesses. In brief, it appears that Olof Jonsson has made the card dematerialize, then rematerialize in an incredible demonstration of mind over matter.

The card does not always make it back into the deck, however. Once I found the card under a chessboard, where it had materialized without disturbing the assembled pieces. During one experiment, the card was discovered in the coat pocket of a witness who had been observing the demonstration at quite some distance from the table where the selection had been made. In another performance, the chosen card was located under the cushion of a couch where a lady of rather heroic proportions had been seated for the entire duration of the experiment. And in several demonstrations, the cards never returned at all. Olof Jonsson has many friends and skeptical challengers who possess a deck of cards with one missing card.

Cary Caraway sent me a report which would seem to offer

evidence of Olof Jonsson's astonishing ability to manipulate an object by dematerializing it and rearranging its very atoms. According to Caraway, the two of them had met for lunch at the Palmer House early in December, 1970. They were seated opposite one another at a dining table when they decided to try to match ESP cards.

"I handed Olof my deck," Caraway said, "and he selected one each of the five symbols for himself—a star, a cross, a square, a circle, and the wavy lines—and the same for me."

Each of the men shuffled their five cards (Caraway taking the added precaution of shuffling his under the table), then, simultaneously, they removed the top card from their mini-decks and placed them in front of themselves on the table.

Olof's first card matched the symbol on Caraway's.

The second set of cards matched.

The third pair matched.

The fourth pair matched.

But the fifth pair *did not* match.

Caraway started to pick up his cards when suddenly he realized the impossibility of what had just happened. If four sets of cards had been matched in simultaneous withdrawals (a procedure which is, in itself, most remarkable), then the fifth pair of cards would have to match.

"I examined my cards and found that I had two squares," Caraway stated in his report. "I assumed that Olof must have erred and given me two squares instead of a cross. I put one square back into the deck, which was on top of the table and over to one side, and took the proper symbol. Now I knew that I had one each of the five symbols."

The men made two more runs, attempting to match the sets, shuffling the cards between each run. They never matched more than three. Then they made the following incredible run:

Caraway's first card was a cross—so was Olof's.

The second pair did not match.

The third pair did not match.

Caraway's fourth card was a cross. . . .

The puzzled architect suddenly recalled that his *first* card had been a cross. Since they were experimenting with five cards, one each of each symbol, this could not be.

"I told Olof this and to prove it I picked up the three top

cards from my stack—we had each stacked our cards in front of ourselves. Olof then looked at his cards and verified that his first card had also been a cross. Now there were three crosses; yet we had begun playing with two crosses—one each!" Caraway said.

"Meanwhile," he went on, "with four cards spread out in my hands and with the fifth card (the cross) still on the table in front of me, I began to reconstruct and explain to Olof the circumstances wherein I had the two squares and had put one back so that I would know that I had one card of a kind.

"Suddenly Olof exclaimed, 'The cross is not a cross any more.' I glanced back at my so-called 'cross' on the table, and it was a star! With this star, I again had one of a kind."

Cary Caraway concludes his report by stating: "I believe this event can only be explained by what we *don't know* about psychic phenomena."

"Olof," I asked, "when you make a card disappear, what do you do with it? Is it suspended in another dimension for a while?"

Olof Jonsson: I think that it does go to another dimension. I cannot really say how I send it there, though, but I can *feel* when I am able to do it. Sometimes I get the feeling just a few moments before an experiment, then I know that I will be able to make a card disappear. I tell someone to think of a card, and once I receive an impression of that card, I send it some other place. Then I tell them to look through the deck and see if it is there. It will be gone.

I can do this with a flower, too. Or anything, if I have the right feeling.

"What happens inside you when you transport something to another dimension?"

Jonsson: I feel very, very tired afterward. I feel like energy has been taken from me, and I will be tired for a little while— maybe ten, fifteen minutes, sometimes longer. . . . It depends on the conditions and the experiment.

"Would it help if you had anything to eat or drink just before the experiment?"

Jonsson: I prefer not to eat too much before an experiment.

"How about afterward?"

Jonsson: Afterward I eat normally. There is one thing that I have noticed when I am doing these experiments, and that is I feel thirsty. There might be some clue there.

"Do you think something may 'evaporate'?"

Jonsson: It's possible, *ja*. The plasma-energy may be working better if I drink water. But more important than water is the proper condition for meditation.

It is important that I be rested and calm. I usually achieve this state after only a few moments, because I can see how wonderful is the world that exists outside this physical world. This knowledge puts the minor distractions of this Earth plane in their proper perspective and makes me calm and peaceful wherever I may be.

When this great calm and peace fills my body, I know that I can do these things. I know that I achieved harmony with the Cosmic powers of the Universe.

"There is an account of an experiment in Sweden during which you made a flower dematerialize, then rematerialize in a friend's home on the other side of the city. Did you just look at the flower and think that you were going to make it disappear?"

Jonsson: Let me say that I did not know where the flower had gone until a friend called a few days later and told of the mysterious occurrence they had had in their home when a flower dropped in the middle of their table from out of nowhere. I told them about the experiment, and they permitted those who had been present to enter their home and examine the flower in order to verify the teleportation.

"So you did not, in this case, have it in your mind to move the flower from this place to that place?"

Jonsson: No, I was sitting before the flower and I got a strong feeling that it would disappear. My mind was open for it. I was in just the right condition for it.

"How could you make the conditions right if they did not exist?"

Jonsson: I would have to meditate until I made the conditions right. For all phases of "psi" I achieve the proper condition with meditation. I release the irritations in my mind and banish the things that disturb me. I attain peace and calm. I achieve harmony.

It is more important to relax the mind than it is the body. You must practice day after day and try to think that nothing will bother you now... you are in another state of consciousness. You can talk to yourself like this and tell yourself to be calm and peaceful and that nothing will bother you, because whatever is within you is more important than the distractions without. Once you learn that, you will feel psychic energy building up within you and you will become calmer and more peaceful.

"Let us say, just to make a hypothetical situation, that in this room there is a flower that you must make disappear. It is a matter of utmost urgency that you cause the flower to disappear. But within this room are people talking loudly, and over in the corner there are some little children and they're tired and irritable and they're quarreling and fighting. A group of inebriated men are laughing and singing in another corner, and almost right at your elbow there is a man cracking walnuts. How, in that environment, would you create the proper peaceful conditions?"

Jonsson: The first thing that I would do would be to erase all the irritations and distractions. Within moments they would not bother me at all, and I can achieve such a state of inner peace that you could drop a bomb outside the window and I wouldn't react. You see, I am no longer in this world; I am in another dimension. I put my arm, my mind, into another dimension so that I can accomplish these things.

"Is this the same dimension where our soul goes when we die?"

Jonsson: Perhaps. "Dimension" may be the wrong word for it. I must answer carefully, because I more often feel the condition than I do the dimension. Everything is conditioned by mind. Everything is mind.

"How might one acquire access to this higher dimension?"

Jonsson: First, meditate and achieve that condition of calm and peace, that cosmic harmony. Then, when the transcendent level of your mind reaches up to the higher laws, you will know what you wish to know.

But remember, you have to convince yourself that you can do anything. The main thing is to convince yourself that you can do it.

It seems that a sense of humor is possible even among these "higher laws." As the Jonssons and the Steigers dawdled over dessert at Johnny Lattner's restaurant in Chicago's Marina Tower, Betty told this anecdote of a mischievous bit of teleportation:

"I was in the kitchen doing dishes, and Olof was sitting there at the table riffling through a deck of cards," she said. "I wasn't particularly interested in doing any experiments, but he wanted to try an. . ."

"It was just the right condition," Olof interrupted. "I could feel the right condition."

"Well, anyway," Betty continued, "he asked me to pick five cards at random from the deck. After I had done this, he asked me to select two cards out of the five. I pointed to the king of clubs and the queen of diamonds. Next, he asked me to shuffle all five cards, then place them on the table and put my hands over them."

"I did not touch them at any time," Olof reminded Betty.

"No," she admitted, "he didn't. I had my hands over what I thought were the five cards. When I picked them up again, the king and the queen were gone. 'Where did they go?' I asked him. That night I had a white shirt-type blouse on, and I had turned back to wash some more dishes when I felt something creeping up inside my bra! Here were the two cards! They just sort of materialized, and I pulled them out of my bra. Olof thought that was pretty funny!"

"I felt so calm and peaceful that night," Olof explained after the laughter had died down at the table. "When I have that feeling, there is a kind of pulsation within me and I know that I can do anything I wish to do. I can do any experiment in telepathy devised by the strictest parapsychologist; I can apport any object I choose. On this night, I thought that it would be more interesting for Betty if the cards would materialize on her own body. I could see through her and watch the cards appearing."

"You were looking through her as if she were transparent?" I questioned, wanting to be certain I understood as much of the mysterious process as possible.

"*Ja,*" Olof said, nodding his head. "I could see the cards as they were forming. One minute there were no cards there, then in the next instant they were beginning to form. And they were the two cards that she had in mind."

"Forgive me for even thinking this," Marilyn had to say, "but what if something had distracted your mood? Could the cards have materialized *inside* Betty?"

Olof's smile remained unaltered, but his mood became at once serious. "Never. The natural laws would not allow such a thing to happen."

Of all the "psi" phenomena that are virtually under Olof Jonsson's mental control, he considers teleportation the most unusual, the most difficult to manage. "Telekinesis is not so unusual for me, because it happens so often," he once told this author. "But a really dramatic apport happens only a few times a year, and most of the time it happens rather spontaneously.

"Something inside me says, 'Now it will happen! I will be looking at something, a flower, a vase, a book, and it will disappear. And I feel strangley different at that time."

Has Olof ever tried conscious apports of substantial material objects?

"Yes, I have tried on occasion to make a jar or a dish to disappear on command when the *feeling* has not been present, but I have been successful only when I have meditated and created the proper conditions," the psychic answered.

"Teleportation presents me with the greatest challenge among 'psi' phenomena. But I know that there is a natural law at work, and someday, when I am meditating, I will achieve the right condition and I will learn that law. Then I will be able to teleport objects twenty-five out of twenty-five times, just as now I am able to name correctly twenty-five out of twenty-five ESP cards through clairvoyance."

Chapter Eighteen

MARRIAGE AND MEDIUMSHIP

There is one rather amusing common factor that I have found in all but a very few of the great psychics; they seem to be quite forgetful, almost absentminded, when it comes to their personal lives. I am not for one moment suggesting that they suffer memory lapses in regard to the problems of those who may consult with them. On the contrary, they may remember word-for-word conversations with consultees that took place years ago. But ask them some detail about their private lives or invite them to lunch, and unless they have an alert spouse or secretary, you may have a long wait before you receive either the requested information or the desired company.

Betty Jonsson does a wonderfully efficient job of running interference for Olof, making certain that he is always where he has promised to be at the agreed time. Such a job is not without its hazards. Olof is such a genial, polite, and charming man that even if the Jonssons together committed the most outrageous social *faux pas*, it would somehow appear to all eyes that Betty alone was responsible for the *gaffe* and that Olof was but an innocent bystander.

"So many people have the wrong ideas about psychics," Betty said once. "Some people think that they are supernatural beings who never err. Olof has his human side just like everyone else. I've seen Olof do things at home when they don't count, when they're not really for anyone. Things have disappeared. Objects have flown around the room. No one could ever convince me that Olof used fraud. Why should he try to impress me after three years of marriage? If anyone ever says anything to me about trickery, they'll have to fight a battle."

Then, after the momentary fire in the dark eyes had cooled, Betty spoke very softly: "I feel that my life has changed a lot since I married Olof. I have a completely different attitude about everything. I may still have some of the same problems, but I am more aware of the problems and how to deal with them. I'm aware of the importance of trying to overcome and correct them. It takes a long time to change attitudes that you've held over a period of many years. You can't just change overnight. But I can feel myself beginning to change my complete way of thinking. It is the beginning of a new time in my life. It's just like my life is beginning to start now, like I've been reborn."

The above tribute to her psychically talented husband was delivered by Betty Jonsson as she and Olof, Arlene Ursitti, my wife, Marilyn, and I sat over coffee and tea after a Sunday brunch at our home in Decorah, Iowa, on an autumn morning. Most of the material in the edited transcript which follows was recorded during that conversation or while conducting a very long, late-night interview during a summer holiday in Wisconsin.

"That was a marvelous tribute you just paid your husband, Betty. You feel, then, that you can take ghostly gray ladies walking in high heels in your daughter's bedroom and cups and saucers floating off your table in stride in view of the more meaningful things that have happened to you since your marriage to Olof?"

Betty Jonsson: Yes. I think Olof is a source of energy for these manifestations, but I know he wouldn't ever willfully hurt anybody or anything. I surely can't blame him for the spontaneous psychic phenomena which have occurred in his presence, but I have benefited much more from his love than I have been frightened by his psychism.

"Have you ever felt, though, that Olof might, on occasion,

manipulate you psychically so that you do things his way?"

Mrs. Jonsson: (Laughing) I have my suspicions every now and then. For example, once Olof wanted to attend a lecture that I had no intention of attending. Olof did not argue with me when I told him that I would absolutely not accompany him. Yet for some reason, I found myself at that lecture. I had suddenly changed my mind at the last moment and decided to attend. Later on, I had the creepy feeling that Olof had done something to change my mind.

The same kind of thing happened when we were invited to a New Year's Eve party. Olof hates New Year's Eve parties, but I insisted that we attend this party. I really wanted to go. So, again, Olof didn't argue. He said that if I wished to go, we would go.

That night I got all dressed up and was really excited. Then, all of a sudden, I became terribly sleepy. I said that I would lie down and rest for just a few minutes and then we would leave for the party. And that is the last that I remember before waking up the next morning. Olof said that he tried to wake me, but I have my suspicions that he was the cause of my long winter's nap!

"Betty, I'll bet that one of the most frequent questions that people ask you is this: 'If Olof can really do all of these things, why isn't he a millionaire?'

Mrs. Jonsson: Oh, you're absolutely right. And it is strange, but there seems to be some natural law that does not permit a psychic to use his talent to further his own financial interests. I have seen Olof do many things that have made other people better off financially or health-wise, yet he has never been able to do any particularly dramatic thing for me in that area.

Olof Jonsson: Oh, yes, Betty. I married you!

Mrs. Jonsson: (Laughing) But this natural law seems to hold true for the other psychics whom we know well. They seem unable to do a great deal for either themselves or their families.

"Perhaps the emotions enter in and distort things. It is very difficult to be objective about one's own body and his own loved ones."

Mrs. Jonsson: People think I have this power at my

fingertips, but Olof will seldom even give me a reading. If I want an in-depth reading, I have to go see Ruth Zimmerman or somebody.

Jonsson: If I got into her life, I would also be getting into my own. I could read for Betty, and I do give her psychic impressions if I feel it is really needful. But then, I read for Ruth and her family and for other psychics, so we have a kind of psychic exchange.

"But you don't give many psychic readings, do you, Olof, even for friends?"

Mrs. Jonsson: No, and when he does give them, he never asks for money. He only wants to see that what he does is appreciated.

Jonsson: I do not care about money as long as I can do something good. I am happy when I know my words have had special meaning to someone in the same manner that a schoolteacher is happy when the students know what he is talking about.

"Betty, have you always been interested in psychical research and the occult?"

Mrs. Jonsson: For about fifteen years now I have been making quite a study of the literature in the field. Actually, I met Olof through a girl friend who told me that she had been going to a good psychic. She introduced me to this mystery man and Olof and I became friends. Then he began to ask me out for dinner and pretty soon the interest became more than the occult—it became the man.

Jonsson: What else could I do when you said that you were hungry?

Mrs. Jonsson: (Laughing) Well, if I remember correctly, I hardly ate a thing that first date.

"Were you afraid the food had been enchanted?"

Mrs. Jonsson: I was just so nervous that I could hardly eat.

You know, when most people see Olof give a demonstration for the first time, they conclude that Olof can read their minds every minute that he is around them. This is what I thought, too.

And then I had these silly little thoughts that he could see through my clothes, and this kind of distrubed me a little, too. I mean, did I wear my pretty undies tonight?

I later found out, of course, that Olof doesn't have his antennas raised all the time. It's just not practical. But if there are a dozen people in a room watching Olof do experiments, nearly every one of them is going to be thinking that Olof is trying to get inside his head and pick his mind apart.

"Betty, once you told me that you experienced some poltergeist manifestations in your apartment during your courtship with Olof."

Mrs. Jonsson: Yes, they would begin about an hour before he would arrive for a date. At the time I thought that Olof was totally responsible for these manifestations, but now that I have read more about such matters, I have learned that being in love and adjusting to one another can add to this type of phenomena. But since strange things continue to happen around our place, Olof must have a great deal to do with them.

"What kind of strange things?"

Mrs. Jonsson: Well, on two occasions, I have had books simply disintegrate, disappear right in my hands, right before my eyes. The first time this happened, I took all the cushions off the couch and slid my hand all around. I had the couch almost completely apart and I could see down the sides to the floor. That book just wasn't there. Olof and I both looked. Then I sat down and resigned myself to the fact that the book was gone. I put my hand down behind the couch once more and I could actually feel something forming in my hand. When I jerked my hand up, I held the book.

Jonsson: It had been transported into another dimension.

"When was the other time that you had a book disappear before your eyes?"

Mrs. Jonsson: It was one day when I had the day off and Arlene [Ursitti] and I went downtown to the art institute and I went into this bookstore that sells secondhand books. You know, Olof doesn't like secondhand books because he can feel the vibrations of previous owners, and sometimes these vibrations upset him. Then, too, he feels that this particular bookstore is in a rough neighborhood and he doesn't like me to go there unescorted.

Anyway, I bought this particular book and Arlene and I went home on an early train. I had not been home long when Olof called on the telephone and said, "Why did you go to that bookstore when I told you never to go there alone? And why did you buy that book?"

I had not told him that I would go to the bookstore that day, so I asked him what made him think that I had been there. "I went there looking for you in my astral body and I saw you there and you bought such-and-such a book," he told me. "Why did you buy a secondhand book? You know how the vibrations upset me."

Well, that's fine for him, but secondhand books don't bother me at all. But I had to admit that I had been at the bookstore and I had purchased the book that he had named.

Then, between the time he hung up and the time he caught the train for home, the book disappeared—right out of its sack! I had looked at it on the train with Arlene, so I knew that it had been there only moments before.

As soon as I picked Olof up at the depot, I started to jump all over him. I asked him if he had had anything to do with the book disappearing. I told him that I had paid for that book and I wanted it returned.

Jonsson: Consciously, I was irritated with Betty for having gone to that bookstore and for buying that book, but my subconscious had taken care of things for me.

"But you did bring it back?"

Mrs. Jonsson: He brought it back that same night, but he must have been really charged with psychic power and anger, because when he went in to take his shower, a cup and saucer left the table in the kitchen and sailed across the room. Disappearing books and floating cups and saucers were just a little bit too much for me all in one day.

"Speaking of showers, Olof really enjoys them, doesn't he?"

Mrs. Jonsson: Does he! He even showers his eyeballs.

Jonsson: I think it is good to bathe often. I think I absorb some kind of energy from the water. If I can, I like to have four or five showers a day. I like water. I like to be clean. I use soap with hot water, then I finish with ice-cold water.

"Do you ever take tub baths?"

Mrs. Jonsson: He will *never* take a tub bath.

"Betty, how do you go about buying a Christmas present for a clairvoyant?"

Mrs. Jonsson: Oh, he makes me so angry at Christmas. He

always knows what I buy for him. At least he could pretend that he was surprised.

Last Christmas, I had picked up several things before Christmas Eve, but on the way home from work that night, I thought that I would buy him one special thing at the very last minute to surprise him. I bought him a red cardigan sweater, and I was no sooner inside the door when he said: "Oh, you bought something red today. I believe you have bought a red sweater for me." Clairvoyance can be a sneaky way of peeking!

"How does Olof sleep at night? Is he a restless sleeper?"

Mrs. Jonsson: Sometimes he tosses a lot, and he'll start speaking in Swedish.

Jonsson: (Laughing) Yes, I now think in English, but I still dream in Swedish. And when I was visiting Sweden last summer, I dreamed in English.

Mrs. Jonsson: There was one time, though, that really frightened me. Olof had gone into a trance state while sleeping. He usually sleeps on his side, but this time he was on his back and his mouth was open and he was speaking in what seemed to be an Oriental tongue. I turned on the light, and he didn't even look like himself. He looked Chinese. It was really frightening.

"Do you ever share dreams?"

Mrs. Jonsson: Oh, yes. Usually the dreams will not be identical in every detail, of course, but they'll be close enough and on the same subject to allow us to know that we blended telepathically during the sleep state.

"Olof, have you always worn the brightly colored clothing that you seem to favor today?"

Jonsson: Yes, only years ago it was not as much in style as it is today.

Mrs. Jonsson: When we visited Sweden last summer, the people would turn and look at him. The women there dress in high fashion, but the men are still pretty conservative. It was kind of amusing. They didn't know Olof could understand Swedish, so they would comment on his manner of dress right in front of him.

Jonsson: At one place we went, they said, "He's either a Dane or an American." I walked up to them and said, "No, I'm Swedish." They were really surprised.

"Betty, have there been any times when Olof has tuned in on

you from his office or when he's riding the commuter train home that you particularly remember?"

Mrs. Jonsson: I'll never forget the occasion just after we had been married when a letter for Olof arrived from Sweden. At that time I did not know any of Olof's relatives and since Olof is not very open about his personal background, it often crossed my mind that I would not know whom to contact in the event that something should happen to him. So I just copied down the address on a piece of paper and put it in my wallet. Olof was not home at that time. He was still on the train.

As soon as he arrived home, he asked, "Is there any mail for me?"

I told him that he had a letter from Sweden, and he said: "Why did you copy down the address?"

I thought, well, it could be a lucky guess, so I did not say anything. Then he said, "You were sitting in such-and-such a chair and you took the paper and folded it in this manner," and he went on to imitate my actions. "Then you took your finger," he went on, "and you poked it down into your wallet." And he imitated me in exactly the manner that I had done this. I was speechless. Then Olof laughed and said: "I know your motives were good; I know why you did it."

Thank goodness my husband is good-natured!

"Olof, how were you able to tune in on Betty on that occasion?"

Jonsson: I was just sitting on the train, allowing my mind to travel about, when I picked up a random thought from Betty: "This is what I am going to do." So I decided that I should see just what it was that she had decided to do. I meditated and I saw everything that she did. I saw how she folded the paper and pushed it in her wallet.

"Just as if you were watching it on a television set."

Jonsson: Yes, and just as clear.

"Betty, what would you say to all those women who may envy your living with a twentieth-century Merlin?"

Mrs. Jonsson: (Laughing) I am always amused by both men and women who approach Olof with that attitude. I mean, Olof is my husband, and I love him very dearly, but I don't believe that he is my savior come down to earth on a velvet cloud. And Olof never consciously tries to give that impression to anyone. The most essential thing that I have learned from Olof is to rely upon the powers within me that link me to a greater intelligence without.

Chapter Nineteen

USING HYPNOSIS TO EXPLORE
THE UNKNOWN AND TO HEAL

Olof Jonsson is convinced that one can establish a source of power and unsuspected strength through hypnotism, but he is equally convinced that: "When hypnotism is employed as a variety show entertainment for a paying audience, one is on dangerous ground. It is because of these often silly demonstrations that medical boards and many doctors become wary of, and even antagonistic toward, everything that bears the hint of hypnotism."

In 1946, Olof worked for the late Dr. Gunnar Nordgren at his clinic in Stockholm, Sweden. "In collaboration with Dr. Nordgren, I was able to accomplish many practical applications of hypnosis and suggestion," Jonsson remarked. "The medical profession in Sweden is, as a unit, as set against the use of hypnosis in therapy and healing as is the medical profession in the United States. However, Dr. Nordgren was exceptionally skilled in the use of hypnosis in the environment of a clinic designed to promote rest and confidence."

Dr. Nordgren and Olof Jonsson had many long discussions wherein they agreed on the great responsibility incumbent upon the hypnotist in any kind of medical therapy. "Dr. Nordgren was of the opinion that medical hypnosis should always be carried on under a doctor's control, regardless of the skill of the hypnotist," Olof remembers. "Less consequential therapy and lighter uses of suggestion, on the other hand, may be entirely safe if they are administered with discrimination."

In all cases in which Olof has employed hypnosis to affect an improvement in health, the individuals were referred to him by medical doctors. "I have been able to bring about excellent results in a wide variety of cases," Jonsson states. "In Dr. Nordgren's clinic, I saw a total of 20,000 people, on an average of thirty-five people a day.

"I remember one instance in which a man had been paralyzed, unable to walk for several years. I relaxed him, placed him into a deep sleep. I told him: 'Now great power shall come to you. Your mind is working to heal you and it is able to draw upon all the healing power of the universe. You will be able to walk!'

"Twenty minutes later," Olof said, "the man began to rise, then he began to walk while still under my hypnotic control. When I wakened him, the 'cure' remained, and he was able to walk down the clinic's steps unassisted."

Olof stressed that he will never consider hypnotic therapy unless it is in collaboration with a medical doctor. "I have always felt a great responsibility for the ability which I possess. I insist that anyone with whom I am to work in this capacity be examined by a medical doctor both before and after a hypnotic session with me."

Dr. J. Bjorkhem, a Swedish physician who conducted several years of research into the medical implications of hypnosis, once stated that hypnosis as an instrument of healing is not to be overlooked. "In a number of nervous conditions, hypnosis can grant unparalleled relief and calm. Hypnosis can sometimes serve as an effective cure for alcoholism. There is no difficulty in demonstrating that hypnosis can effect painless tooth extraction. With some pregnant women, one can, occasionally, by means of hypnosis, establish a specific time for delivery and accomplish a painless birth. For one who has ventured to develop the powers of hypnosis fully, it is not unusual for him to be able to bring about hypnotic phenomena even by telephone."

Olof Jonsson has achieved telephone hypnosis on innumerable occasions with great success. It is not always necessary for the subject concerned to be aware of what is about to take place. In fact, it is often better if he is oblivious to the planned experiment, in order to eliminate skeptical accusations that the subject may only be pretending to be in trance or may have placed himself in hypnotic sleep by autosuggestion.

Some sensitive people have fallen asleep just by hearing Olof's voice. On certain occasions, he has placed people into hypnotic trance without even being near them or telling them about his intentions.

Once at a party in Varberg, Sweden, Olof was challenged to undertake hypnotic experiments without being present in the same room as his subject and without having any personal contact whatsoever with the subject. Jonsson agreed, and the hostess suggested that the subject be a woman who had not yet arrived at the party.

"But would Mrs. Bjerke object to my hypnotizing her?" Olof wanted to know. "I would not wish to interfere with her free will. It is my impression that she would not mind being the unknowing subject in such an experiment. Can anyone counter this?"

"Not at all," the hostess, Mrs. Lundquist, said, "she has often expressed her willingness to be hypnotized by Engineer Jonsson. More than once over coffee we have discussed her curiosity about hypnotism. I am certain that she would have no objection."

Two young doctors, Dr. Mikkelson and Dr. Fardahl, stated that they would support the experiment as controllers. Olof Jonsson told the party that when Mrs. Bjerke arrived, he would immediately disappear into the kitchen. There would then be two rooms and two doors between him and his subject.

"When the lady sits in that armchair in front of the drapes," Olof informed the party, "I guarantee that she shall fall asleep within two seconds."

Twenty minutes later, when Mrs. Bjerke rang the doorbell, Olof took his immediate leave of the front room. Mrs. Bjerke exchanged greetings with everyone present, then was shown to the armchair in front of the drapes.

She had barely managed to sit down before her head fell forward on her breast and she slept deeply and quietly. Doctors Mikkelson and Fardahl approached, felt her pulse, lifted her head to be certain that her sleep was sound. The doctors tried to rouse the woman, but they were unable to penetrate the cloud of hypnotic sleep with which Jonsson had swathed her.

When Olof was brought back into the room, he walked directly to the entranced woman and stood before her chair. "You are calm and composed," he told her. "It was good that you should sleep a bit so that you might enjoy the party even more. Wake up!"

Mrs. Bjerke awakened at once, stretched contentedly, and asked the party to forgive her her unprecedented lapse of manners, but she had just enjoyed the most delightful sleep. When the hostess presented Olof Jonsson to Mrs. Bjerke, the awakening sleeper laughed and understood at once the connection.

"So I was the subject of a little experiment, eh?" she smiled. "Well, Engineer Jonsson, I do not mind. I have not felt so lively and rested for a long time!"

When Olof visited Australia in 1951, he came into contact with a number of people interested in parapsychology. They took his experiments seriously and did everything they could to facilitate his investigations. Jonsson remembers especially the interested cooperation which he received from the press. When Sydney's highly respected newspaper *The Sunday Sun* asked him to conduct an experiment in telephone hypnosis from their offices, Jonsson accepted without hesitation.

"The experiment was arranged under reliable supervision," Olof recalled for me recently. "I was placed in the editor's office at the *Sunday Sun* and my subjects, two women, were watched by reporters and photographers in a big warehouse in the Imperial Arcade."

According to the *Sunday Sun* for March 4, 1951:

The telephone rang. Miss Thorpe lifted the receiver and answered. Sixty seconds later she was asleep. She held the receiver firmly in her hand.

During the three minutes she was hypnotized, she sat absolutely motionless. She reacted in no way either to speech or to loud calling. Nor did the photographic flashes disturb her in the least.

When the three minutes were over, someone put the receiver to her ear. She awakened instantly at the sound of Engineer Jonsson's voice.

Miss Thorpe said afterward that she would never forget the words that she heard Engineer Jonsson say over the telephone: "You feel very tired. . .you are closing your eyes. . .you are sleeping." And later: "You feel rested and composed. . .you have slept beautifully. Wake up!"

The experiment with Miss Reed was equally successful. Both women felt very relaxed and calm afterward.

Then Jonsson talked by telephone with the manager of the warehouse. Jonsson had never met this man, but by only hearing his voice he could say his name, his birthday, the year of birth, and also describe his appearance in detail.

"I happened to be in Sydney during an election," Olof told me, "when I found myself in the company of some friends in a big park where one of the radical party's foremost speakers was fulminating with blistering oratory. My friends wondered whether I, for the sake of argument, could not influence the speaker and cause him to become confused.

"I promised to try," Olof chuckled at the memory, "and I went as close to the speaker's stand as possible. I put my tele-hypnosis to work, and as luck would have it, the speaker proved to be of a suggestible nature. At first he became unsure of himself, and after a while, he simply stopped and looked out at the audience as he had forgotten why he had come there that night. Then, taking a deep breath, he began to speak with as much zeal as before—for the benefit of his principal political opponent!"

On another occasion, Olof stopped at a shop in Stockholm so that his companion, Mrs. Spilde, the wife of a friend, might buy a pack of cigarettes. The clerk happened to be one of those haughty women who enjoys making her customers feel as if she is doing them a favor by waiting on them. Perhaps, Olof reasoned, if the clerk were momentarily unable to perform even the simplest of tasks, she might be reminded that she was, after all, as frail and finite a human being as those she deigned to wait upon.

Mrs. Spilde asked for a certain brand of cigarettes, and the clerk only sniffed by way of response. It appeared to Olof and his companion that the woman walked toward the cigarette rack as if she had been asked to fetch a loathsome reptile from a bucket of slime. She stood before the tobacco shelves for a long while, then she returned to her customers empty-handed.

"I. . .I seem to have forgotten which brand of cigarettes you requested," she admitted, dropping the words slowly from her lips.

Mrs. Spilde repeated her order, and the clerk turned on her heel to fulfill the request. Olof could hardly suppress his mirth when, once again, the haughty clerk stood puzzled and dazed before the tobacco shelves. For long moments she remained there, her eyes studying each brand of cigarettes, cigars, and pipe tobacco.

"I'm terribly sorry," she apologized to her customers as she rejoined them at the counter. "Would. . .would you mind repeating that brand, please?" A small, almost winsome smile appeared suddenly on her lips. She was trying her best to shield her confusion behind a smile that begged for their sympathy and understanding.

On her third try, she returned triumphant, the requested pack of cigarettes held proudly—but not haughtily—in her hand. "Strange I couldn't see them before," she laughed. "Goodness, they were right there on the shelf in front of me. And they're one of our most popular brands, too!"

As they left the shop, Mrs. Spilde turned to Olof and whispered: "You never stop your bewitching, do you?"

Sune Stigsjoo, a Swedish publisher, told of the time that he and Olof were left stranded at their table by an unattentive waiter. "The man was at the far end of the restaurant engaged in deep conversation with a co-worker. He neither heard nor saw any of his customers, and we had sat for more than fifteen minutes waiting to pay our bill.

"'Can't you use suggestion to get that waiter over here?' I asked my friend Jonsson.

"'I shall try,' came the answer. He placed one hand on top of the other, then he cast a sharp glance at the two men far off in the corner. There was not a second's delay before our waiter looked as if he had been hit by a bolt of electricity. Without a word to his co-worker, he made his way directly to our table, moving for all the world like a sleepwalker. When he arrived at our table, he looked just a little embarrassed, almost as if he did not know precisely what he had to do with our table."

Now and then Olof Jonsson experimentally deadens a portion of his own body's receptivity to pain. One such demonstration usually makes a strong impression on observers. Stepping up to a sturdy table, Jonsson brings his arm down with great force and strikes the outside edge of his hand on the sharp side of a table leaf. Once an illustrated newspaper accused Olof of turning his hand unnoticeably and striking its inner side on the edge of the table. "Anyone at all can do that!" the newspaper suggested.

"Such an explanation is thoroughly incorrect," Olof told me. "I now color the outside of my hand with lipstick and place a white paper on the table exactly where my hand will strike. The lipstick imprints its color on the paper, furnishing sufficient proof that nothing in the demonstration is faked."

I have seen Olof perform his lack-of-sensitivity experiments on several different occasions. Jonsson is a solidly built man and he is able to bring the edge of his hand down on a table's side with a vigor reminiscent of a karate expert. But regardless of how loudly the *thwack* sounds as flesh meets wooden surface, there is never any mark on Jonsson's hand and never any indication of pain mirrored in his face.

A news story in Sweden's *Varbergposten* reported how Olof had removed the pain that a Miss Anna-Lise Jacobson had endured for three years. In view of the fact that Jonsson completely obliterated all traces of discomfort within a minute's time, one can only ponder the enormous reserves of curative powers which must lie latent in everyone's psyche.

Miss Jacobson, who worked in a bank, told the press that she believed that she might have acquired the terrible pain in her hands and arms from too much mechanical bookkeeping. "Heretofore neither doctor's treatments, radio vibrations, massage, rest, nor immobility had helped," she stated. "I can only say what the situation is now: now the pain is gone. It is quite unbelievable, but true. It is marvelous."

"When I tried to help Miss Jacobson in this way," Olof was quoted as saying, "I set her back a thousand years in time in order that she might go into a sufficiently deep sleep and be freed of the pain. I learned a great deal which is useful in such situations from a close study of the methods of primitive peoples, especially from the Indians in South America."

Another story in a Swedish newspaper recounts the case of a man who had for several years suffered from a knotted tendon in the inside of his hand. Through the effects of the constant tension and lack of exercise, his fingers had become stiff, useless. A doctor present at the demonstration examined the patient and could only recommend an operation.

Then, according to the newspaper account: "Jonsson put the man into a hypnotic state, and after a while when he awakened, he could move his fingers without any impairment. In this way, Jonsson has also cured many cases of stuttering, as well as other similar difficulties."

Olof Jonsson's observations on hypnosis:

It is a common misconception that, in order to influence his subject, a hypnotist must look him in the eye. Such a popular notion is, of course, completely false. I can place subjects in hypnotic sleep simply by speaking to them over the telephone or even by asking them to look at my picture. On several occasions, I have hypnotized men and women while separated from them by walls, doors, and several miles.

All of this has nothing to do with hypnosis in the usual meaning of the term, but with a kind of radiation which I project and that no walls in the world can manage to stop. This "radiation," or thought-projected force, has been called, for lack of a more expressive term, "tele-hypnosis." It is also true that there is such a thing as "time-adjusted hypnosis." I can get a person to carry out on a certain day, hour, minute, and second, an order that I have given him in the hypnotic state. It makes no difference whether the execution of this command lies years ahead in time. I have tested this experiment many times and it has never gone wrong. For anyone who doubts me, I shall be happy to demonstrate!

When I am working with hypnosis, I cannot help calling forth the so-called psychic sense which every person has, but which, as yet, only certain persons can make to function at will.

Whenever I hypnotize an individual, I sincerely endeavor to work with a strong sense of responsibility and with that person's welfare foremost in my mind. I have never concealed the fact that more than once when I was younger I considered seriously the idea of shifting saddles and becoming a medical doctor. But my decision, obviously, was to continue to experiment with what man has so long in his ignorance spoken of as the "supernatural."

It seems so long ago since I was that little boy sitting by the stream absorbing my inspiration from some mystical source, which I only much later analyzed as the Cosmic. It has been a never-ending challenge to attempt to translate into mere words what really occurs in mystical experiences, hypnotic sleep, the trance state, meditation. Although it is extremely difficult to word mystical experiences intelligibly, it is, however, a mistake to say that a mystic in ecstasy does not experience anything. It is only that he cannot express it understandably.

Chapter Twenty

THE PSYCHIC EVIDENCE FOR REINCARNATION

The young man sat slumped in his chair, speaking in a soft monotone that had begun to accelerate and take on more dramatic fluctuations in voice pattern. Then his eyes widened in fear and he gripped the arms of the large chair in which he sat: "They swarm over the ship!" he screamed. "Drive them back into the sea! Kill them!"

Olof Jonsson moved forward. "You will relax," he told the young man. "You will be able to see things in a more detached manner. You will be able to tell us everything that is happening around you, but you will feel no fear, feel no pain."

The hypnotized subject was describing an ostensible past life that he had lived as a Dane in about the year 892. He had already told Jonsson and the assembled experimenters that he had lived in Jylland and had been a fisherman by trade. He had a wife, quite plump, and six children. He was called Sten the Weakling, not because of a lack of physical strength, but because he was regarded as a bit mentally slow by his fellows. As a Viking warrior, however, he had distinguished himself in many rugged battles. Now, as his unseen audience listened in silence, "Sten" described the last battle of his life.

"Over the sides with the swine!" he shouted amidst wild battle cries. He and his Danish comrades were doing battle with a marauding Swedish longship, and it was a vicious encounter with members of one tribe of Vikings pitted against another. "By Odin! Feed the swine to the fish!"

In mid-shout, the young man gasped and clutched his side. He clenched his teeth so that he would not whimper his pain.

"Remember, you will feel no pain," Olof reminded him. "What has happened to you?"

"A spear," he cursed. "A spear from that coward. He came at me from behind, and I turned in time to catch the throw in my side."

"Is it bad?"

"Sten" nodded. "I can hear the song of the Valkyrie. They come to take me to Valhalla. One of the Swedish dogs raises his sword and hacks at my throat, but I do not care. I feel no pain. I have died in battle as a true Viking warrior."

The young man "Sten" released a last breath, and one of the witnesses stepped forward to clutch Olof Jonsson's sleeve. "My god, man!" he whispered hoarsely, "don't let him die!"

Olof assured the witness that he retained control of the personality. "Sten," Olof said to the dying man, "tell us what happens now—after the state known as physical death."

"I s-seem. . ."

"Yes?" Olof prompted after several moments of silence from "Sten."

"I seem to be floating," the entity answered. "Just floating in the sky."

"Can you see your body?"

"Yes," the entity answered. "It is right below me. I can see it on the deck of our longship. How strange it seems to see me down there and yet know that I am really up here. My head. . .its head. . .has nearly been chopped away from the neck. There is blood all around. It appears that my comrades are losing. The Swedes are too many for them."

"Can you see any Valkyrie around you?" Olof wanted to know. "Are they taking you to Valhalla?"

"I thought I heard them as I was dying," the entity known as Sten answered, "but I do not see them."

"Is there anyone there with you?"

"I seem to sense other presences," the Viking replied. "But I do not seem to know them. I cannot yet see them too clearly."

"Can you tell anything at all about them?" Olof pursued the matter.

"Only that I seem to sense that they mean me no harm,'" Sten answered.

"Now, Sten, I want you to move through time and space until it is July 15, 1950, ten fifteen P.M. You will be once more in the library of Dr. Petersen of Stockholm, and you will be once more the entity known as Lars Torkelsen," Olof commanded. "By the time that I count to three, you will be back in the present. One, drifting through time and space; two, coming closer and closer; three. . . ."

Olof Jonsson: Before I left Sweden, I had placed nearly one thousand people into hypnotic trance and had led them back to relive what appeared to be their former lives. One young woman gave names which we were able to trace through old church records. She named many members of her family in her former life, and we located old records and deeds to support her apparent memory.

There were many other cases in which a great number of details of an alleged former life were given by a subject, and we were often able to substantiate a good many of these facts. I have also sent subjects back thousands of years, but even though observing historians and investigators may agree that the subject has the flavor of a time, there is no way to check a story that goes back so many years.

"What have you been able to learn about the nature of reincarnation in your research?"

Jonsson: One time when I had a subject in deep trance and had moved him from the death experience to a spiritual plateau between lives, I asked him to talk about how the soul progresses.

He said that around the soul is built a body that later develops until the point of physical death. At that time, the soul continues its wanderings in the world of spirit. A span of about 144 years passes before the soul again takes habitation in a new body, and each soul is reborn on an average of twelve times. After the last incarnation, we become wholly spiritual creatures.

When I asked what it was like to live in the world of spirits between incarnations, he answered that it was wonderful: he felt so in harmony with the Universe.

He also informed me that each soul is reunited with his soulmate, the mate he had in his first incarnation. The soulmate is like one's true "other half," and one will be whole and happy after his final incarnation.

"Although we have previously discussed what awaits man in the afterlife, let us now examine the matter from the viewpoint of reincarnation. Olof, what do you feel happens immediately after the soul leaves the body in physical death?"

Jonsson: I feel that the soul is translated into a higher dimension. In that dimension, the soul will be *born* as spirit, not as body. On this plane we are used to seeing bodies in order to identify a person, but I don't believe that a body structure is necessary in a higher life condition. I feel that the material plane of existence on which we are living now is but a moment in our *real* lives.

"Where does the soul go after physical death?"

Jonsson: The soul leaving the plane of materialism is very much like a voyager leaving the Mainland and venturing out to sea. As time passes, he drifts farther and farther away from the old. After he has docked in a fascinating new world, he becomes less interested in what he has left behind him and becomes more concerned about developing the new opportunities before him. At first, the voyager may feel a bit insecure while he is getting to know new friends and so forth, but when he has established a new home, the old Mainland becomes only a part of his memory.

"Then why reincarnation? Why do people come back to the Mainland?"

Jonsson: Not everyone does. I do not believe that everyone reincarnates, or at least not so often.

I think it is like when the farmer puts a seed into the earth: sometimes the plant grows and sometimes it doesn't. I think it may be the same with souls. Not all of them grow properly.

"And if they do not grow properly, they must be replanted."

Jonsson: Yes.

"Do you believe in Karma?"

Jonsson: Yes, if you mean the Divine Laws of Compensation and the Supreme Law of Spiritual Growth. If you mean Karma as some kind of punishment for the soul, then I do not accept it. I do not accept punishment in the afterlife or in a series of incarnations. I believe that we may have to endure certain kinds of sufferings to learn important lessons, to clear a situation. I do not believe that suffering is meant by Divine Intelligence to be a punishment for sins.

"At what moment do you believe the soul enters the physical body?"

Jonsson: I believe the soul enters the body when the infant takes its first breath of life upon achieving independence from the mother's womb.

"What effect do you think birth control pills might have on the Wheel of Rebirth?"

Jonsson: I don't think birth control pills have any effect at all on reincarnation. If one misses one train, he simply waits for another.

"What about abortion? How might abortion affect reincarnation or Karma?"

Jonsson: I don't think abortion will interfere with reincarnation in any way. If you do not buy one automobile, you may soon be interested in another. If you don't get into one body, you'll get into another.

"What do you think is the ultimate goal of life in view of the spiritual progress of reincarnation?"

Jonsson: I think that what we are working for is not something materialisitic. We are striving to achieve Harmony and a reuniting with the Great Mind and its complete knowledge of the Universe.

Chapter Twenty-One

WHAT AWAITS MAN IN THE AFTERLIFE

"No," Olof Jonsson replied to my question, "you know that I do not believe in death. Oh, of course, there is the physical death, but the spiritual essence survives."

Olof had told me before that he saw the life of the soul as interdimensional, dwelling within a fleshly domicile in our material dimension, graduating to a higher plane upon the physical death of its bone, blood, and tissue.

"I feel more alive when I am in the right condition to read *en clairvoyant* than I do when I am just eating my breakfast toast or working at my drawing board. Why is that? Because I know that my soul-self is more in the higher dimension than it is in the lower dimension with my physical body. When we hold seances, I am able to see the soul-bodies of other people from other dimensions sitting there around us. I cannot talk to them, but I can pick up psychic impressions from them."

I reminded Olof that once he had told me that even before death, our souls exist in more than one dimension.

"Yes, of course. We live in one dimension, but our souls really belong to another. In meditation and in dreams this fact becomes very apparent. It is quite simple for the transcendental element within us to rise to the higher plane of existence. It is really a matter of a rate of personal vibration. If you look at a fan, and it is going very slow, you will be able to see the blades. If the fan is going very fast, then you cannot see the blades. They have become invisible, and you can see through them. So it is with our souls as they begin to 'vibrate' faster and faster. In time they require little effort to pass one from dimension to another."

But how do our souls pass through the "fan"—the barrier between material and spiritual dimensions—without getting chopped to pieces?

"For most souls, this passing through the barrier will be accomplished at the moment of physical death," Olof answered. "The vibrations will be so fast in the next life that we will be able to pass through walls, through concrete, through any physical barrier—like sunlight passes through glass, like heat passes through a steel pipe.

"But as I keep emphasizing, life, existence, is inter-dimensional, and through proper techniques of meditation, man may achieve full consciousness of his true potential before the transition of physical death. When one meditates properly, he learns to flow with the dimensional frequencies and to enter the higher planes of being while his soul still retains residence in the body," Olof continued.

"Of course, if one has allowed his psyche to become crystallized by an excessive interest in material possessions, proper meditation becomes all but impossible to achieve," the psychic went on. "Material objects belong to the lower dimension, and if one cannot release his hold on them, he will find the liberation of his psyche, both before and after physical death, very difficult."

In his discussions with me, Olof Jonsson has repeatedly stressed the importance of meaningful and effective sessions of meditation in which the transcendent level of mind is allowed free reign to move through the higher dimensions freed from bodily concerns. According to Olof, such a meditative state is so valuable because ". . .it will help people to understand that this life really means almost nothing compared to what we can expect in the next life."

It is Olof Jonsson's firm conviction that once one has gained insight into the next state of existence, he has received a valuable perspective that will aid him in living his present life on the material plane much more significantly.

"I believe in everyone living the good life," Olof has said, "but I think we can do so honestly. We don't have to be cruel to one another. When man sees what awaits him in the afterlife, he will regard all the worries of this life to be but petty considerations."

What can man expect in the afterlife?

He can expect to know more about the universe, because he will have more senses than he has now, and he will be able to travel anywhere he desires in an instant.

Will the surroundings in the next world be similar to our earthly environment?

They will be similar, but much more wonderful, more colorful, and richer in texture.

But we ourselves will be mind-soul, rather than physical body.

Yes. Now we see our material world with five senses, and only occasionally do we utilize the transcendent level of consciousness which we call "psi," the sixth sense. In the next world, all souls will have full control of this unknown faculty and their existence will be fuller, richer.

In the next life, we will not have the temptations that we have in this life. There will be no need to steal, for example, because everyone will create with his own mind whatever he desires. Whoever wishes a large castle will build it with his mind. Whatever you want, you will have but to think it and it will be there.

Olof Jonsson's vision of the afterlife is one of pure mind in which the techniques of existence seem very much like the mechanics of a dream. One dreams of an adventure on the open sea, and the marvelous dream machinery supplies full-masted sailing vessels, a complete crew, sea gulls, white-capped waves, and an exotic South Sea island. Can it be that one's life after death may be as personalized as his dream life on the material plane?

A case from Volume VIII of the *Proceedings* of the Society

for Psychical Research recounted the experience of a man who confronted his moment of physical death; had an out-of-body projection; and somehow returned to consciousness and the continuance of his temporal existence.

Dr. Wiltse of Skiddy, Kansas, felt himself to be dying and so bade good-bye to his family and friends. Dr. S. M. Raynes, the physician in attendance, later testified that Dr. Wiltse passed four hours without pulse or perceptible heartbeat.

During this time, Dr. Wiltse had been elevated to a state of "conscious existence" and discovered that he no longer had anything in common with his body. In his new state of consciousness, he began to rock to and fro, trying to break connection with the tissues of the old cumbersome body. He seemed to ". . .feel and hear the snapping of innumerable small cords," and he began to retreat from his feet toward his head "as a rubber cord shortens."

After a few moments of "shortening," Dr. Wiltse "felt" himself in the head, emerging through the sutures of the skull. "I recollect distinctly," he said later, "how I appeared to myself something like a jellyfish as regards color and form."

When he emerged from the skull, Dr. Wiltse floated up and down laterally, like a soap bubble attached to the bowl of a pipe, until he at last broke loose from the body and fell lightly to the floor. At this point, he slowly rose and expanded to the full stature of a man.

"I seemed to be translucent, of a bluish cast, and perfectly naked," Dr. Wiltse writes in his account of the experience.

He decided that he should exit at once and he headed directly for the door. When he reached the door, he found himself suddenly clothed. Two of his friends stood soberly before the door and were completely oblivious to his presence. To Dr. Wiltse's surprise, he found he could pass through them and out of the door.

"I never saw the street more distinctly than I saw it then," he recalled. It was also at this time that Dr. Wiltse noticed that he was attached ". . .by means of a small cord, like a spider's web," to his body in the house. Then, as if magically propelled, the doctor soared into the air and found himself surveying various locales and scenery.

Dr. Wiltse had just begun to enjoy his new freedom when he found himself on a road that had steep rocks blocking his journey. He tried to climb around them, but at that moment "a black cloud descended on me and I opened my eyes to find myself back on my sickbed."

I have long felt that the experience of Dr. Wiltse provides us with a number of excellent tentative answers to the academic, but persistent, questions as to why one who has projected his soul from his body—whether at the time of physical death or in conscious or spontaneous out-of-body projections—should see himself in familiar bodily appearance and should see clothing around that same structure. It is my theory that since out-of-body experience involves the essential stuff of man's personality and is therefore a "psi" phenomenon, the projected mind may, in those cases in which the agent sees a "body" rather than some kind of wispy substance, "create" the clothing by exercising the same kind of mental machinery that is used in dreams. I think the same thing may be true in the afterlife, when the soul has made the "final projection." I employed the case of Dr. Wiltse to illustrate this theory in an earlier work [*The Mind Travellers*, 1968, Award Books, New York], and I feel that it would be helpful to quote that material at this point in our discussion of what awaits man in the afterlife:

> When he first projects from the skull, Dr. Wiltse perceives himself as "something like a jellyfish as regards color and form." Then, because his mind has been conditioned on the temporal plane to think in terms of body concepts, the "jellyfish" expands into the full stature of a naked man. Primitive man may have been content with such an appearance in his out-of-body experiences, but Dr. Wiltse, upon confronting his sober-faced friends at the door to his bedroom, suddenly finds himself clothed. Again, a lifetime on the earthly plane and in a particular culture had conditioned the doctor not to conceive of himself going about in the nude.
>
> I think it is quite likely that once one has made the "ultimate projection," one learns to discard temporal-plane concepts of "body" and "clothing" and becomes quite satisfied with the "shiny cloud," "bright balloon," or "something like a jellyfish" forms of one's soul or essential self.
>
> . . .it is also worth noting in the Dr. Wiltse case that the experience terminated when he was confronted by steep rocks that blocked his

journey. Generally speaking, there seems to be two types of environment for out-of-body experiences:

1.] the environment of this Earth, in which the projected personality observes the actions of people and sees actual occurrences in faraway places, which he can later substantiate; and

2.] the environment of other planes of existence, or dimensions of reality, in which the projected personality may encounter entities, which he interprets as being "angels," "masters," "guides," or the "spirits" of loved ones who have passed away. The geography of these various planes or dimensions seems to be almost precisely that of Earth, and is often [depending upon the religious views of the projector] interpreted as being Heaven. The "rocks" that halted Dr. Wiltse's advance may indeed have been rocks on another plane of existence, or, again, they may have been formed by the doctor's own mental machinery as a symbol that he was not to travel farther, but was to return to his body. Whether such "solid" symbology is necessary after one has become acclimated to another plane of existence, we, of course, have no way of knowing. We are able to base our theorizations only on the testimony of those who have not yet made the "ultimate projection" when death severs the "silver cord."

A former president of the British Society for Psychical Research, H. H. Price, has conjectured that the whole point of our life on earth might be to provide us with a stockpile of memories out of which we might construct an image world at the time of our death. Such a world would be a psychological world and not a physical one, even though it might seem to be a physical world to those who would experience it.

In Volume 5, Number 1 of *Tomorrow*, Price theorizes that the other world "...would be the manifestation in image form of the memories and desires of its inhabitants, including their repressed or unconscious memories and desires. It might be every bit as detailed, as vivid, and as complex as this present perceptible world which we experience now...it might well contain a vivid and persistent image of one's own body. The surviving personality, according to this conception of survival, is in actual fact an immaterial entity. But if one habitually thinks of oneself as embodied [as one well might, at least for a considerable time], an image of one's own body might be, as it were, the persistent center of one's image world, much as the perceived physical body is the persistent center of one's perceptible world in this present life."

"Then," I asked Olof, "if the afterlife is a world of pure mind, or pure soul, one's yearnings and repressed desires might be realized and fulfilled after physical death."

Jonsson: Yes, but we will not long be interested in such things. We will know many more of the secrets of life, the real meaning of existence, so that we will not long be satisfied with building dream castles. We will become more concerned with learning more of the great spiritual lessons of the Universe. It is my impression that in the afterlife there will be another kind of "death," that is, a "transition," which will graduate the soul to an even higher plane of being. We will continue to evolve from plane to plane, on each level vibrating faster and faster, until we shall become pure light, cosmic energy. At that time, we shall have achieved the highest of harmonious states.

"Even then, will we still have personality and intelligence?"

Jonsson: I believe that we belong to a system of universal intelligence. One can splinter off and become an individual any time he likes, even after harmonizing with the Supermind.

"Is there also a system of punishment in the afterlife?"

Jonsson: No. In this life we must have a police force to protect the so-called normal people from those who were born with flaws. It is my philosophy that we have no bad people, only those who are born with abilities or disabilities that differ from others. I believe that we all belong to a Supermind which we may call God, a Supermind that must obey the same universal laws which it has established for the most minute and flawed atom of its whole.

In the afterlife, there is no punishment, no suffering, no good or bad; there is only perfect Harmony

Chapter Twenty-Two

THE STOCK MARKET "GURU" WHO SEES TOMORROW

"There was this man who came to me who was completely unsophisticated in terms of the stock market," Mr. R.L.G., an investment counselor, recalled for me. "Even when everyone else was making money without really trying, he was losing on every investment. I tried to explain some of the nuances of the market to him, but without any marked degree of success.

"Suddenly he began to select stocks that quickly tripled in value. When I asked him how he was doing it, he stammered and admitted that he was seeing a psychic. I asked him, 'A psychic *what?*' I didn't know anything about mystics and psychics at that time. So he told me about Olof Jonsson. I couldn't believe him, but then when I met Jonsson I couldn't believe that such a man could be running around loose. I was surprised some corporation or university laboratory didn't have his brain plugged into a computer. I brought Jonsson out to my home to give a demonstration of his abilities for my friends, who are all professional or academic people. He completely wowed us."

Word of a psychic stock market counselor cannot be confined to a small, select circle of friends and acquaintances. On November 13, 1967, *Newsweek's* "Business and Finance" section ran a report on the "upside-down market" that included the following comment:

> Perhaps the wildest story of the week came out of Chicago, where several dozen investors have been backing stock tips originating with a Swedish-born spiritualist named Olof Johnson [sic]. Johnson runs his finger down a newspaper stock table and, when he gets a special sensation, stops and writes down the name of the stock. Word of his choices has spread by grapevine from one or two of Johnson's friends to the others in the "syndicate."
>
> "I know this is a horrible example of market advice," admits one of Johnson's followers cheerfully, "but boy, I'm staying with this guru." Small wonder. Several months ago, the investor bought Johnson-touted Farrington Manufacturing Co. at $5 a share, recently sold out at $20, and has now plunged into another Johnson stock called United Australian Oil, a penny issue which has almost doubled from 25 cents to 48 cents.

One couple who followed Olof's stock market tips laughed as they recalled that on numerous occasions the psychic would advise them to buy certain companies which the brokers were unaware even existed.

"Sometimes when we bought stocks we would get a letter from the broker or the firm stating that they wished it clearly understood that they did not recommend that we buy that stock, and it was their advice that we *not* buy that stock," Mr. S. told me.

"But," his wife pointed out, "we had stocks that we bought for seventy-five cents go all the way up to sixty dollars. Olof would just sit there with a pencil in his hand, running the tip up and down the columns. When he would receive a strong impression of which stocks would make it, he would tell us which ones to buy."

Mr. S. went on: "One time we were watching Olof on *Kup's Show*, and Irv Kupcinet asked him if he could predict the stock market. Olof says, sure, and starts to name a stock. Kup cut him off by saying that he couldn't have anyone giving the TV audience stock market advice. He didn't want people writing in to complain to him that they had lost their money. But we heard the name of the stock that Olof gave before Kup shut him off, and we went out and bought it and we watched it go up to a nice sixty dollars."

Olof's ability to glimpse the future seems to lie always at the ready, and he need not sit down with a pen over a list of stocks or stretch out and go into trance to contact the transcendent level of his essential self that views all time as an Eternal Now. Loyola University professor James Hurley told Chicago *Tribune Magazine* [August 22, 1965] of the time that he took Olof to meet trial lawyer John D. Hayes in his office on North La Salle Street.

"Hayes, whose legal practice consists primarily of personal injury suits, was awaiting the verdict of a particularly complex case," Hurley writes. "By this time the jury had been deliberating about two hours. It had been an extremely tedious litigation. Hayes was haggard and worn."

Hurley realized that he had chosen the wrong day to introduce Jonsson to the attorney. Perhaps he would have made his apologies and left Hayes to his lonely wait, when the lawyer leaned back in his chair and said: "Olof, if you *can* foretell the future, will my client win, and if so, how much will he be awarded?"

Without hesitation, Jonsson answered: "Your client *will* win, Mr. Hayes. The settlement will be slightly over a hundred thousand dollars."

Hurley remembers that Hayes simply lit another cigarette and smiled sardonically as they left his office. But then:

> Early the next morning, I received a phone call from an excited barrister. Hayes informed me that either Olof was one helluva psychic or else he had been listening at the jury room door. The jury had returned a verdict of $101,000. He then flippantly asked whether my friend wanted to go to Las Vegas.

Early in January, 1970, Bess Krigel, a Chicago-area psychic schoolteacher, who at that time hosted a Saturday morning show, *ESP with Bess,* on WWCA, Gary, Indiana, called me to discuss the possibility of having a "psych-in" on her program.

"Each year you rate the seers' accuracy in *Fate* magazine," she pointed out, "and you state that you can only score those who have either had their predictions published prior to the event or who have had some public declaration of them. Why not invite the area psychics to air their prognostications? That is as good as publishing them, right?"

I conceded that the broadcasting of a prediction constituted documentation of prophecy before the event, and I agreed to attend the broadcast in order to tape the predictions firsthand. A few days later, Bess called to inform me that the show would be aired live on January 10. The guest list of seers read like a virtual *Who's Who* of American psychics: Irene Hughes, Ruth Zimmerman, Joseph DeLouise, Olof Jonsson, Merle Meyer, Mae Darling, Dr. Lasca Bogdanova, Harold Schroeppel, and Milton Kramer.

On the morning of January 10, my wife and I stopped by the Jonssons' apartment for a bit of breakfast before driving to Gary. As Betty set some hot rolls on the table, Marilyn wanted to know which predictions Olof was going to release for broadcast purposes that morning.

Olof sat silently for a few moments before he answered. "I have been wondering how to phrase some of them. For example, I see that Nasser will die this year. Shall I just state it that way? 'Nasser will die in office before the year ends.'"

"Crepe-hanging is never pleasant over the air," I commented. "And in the question of a politician here in the United States it can be very ill-advised. For example, if you said that you saw Nixon being shot at by a sniper, some mentally disturbed malcontent might decide that he is to be the divine fulfillment of your prophecy."

"You think that I should reword that prediction?" Olof asked.

"Why not just say that Nasser will *be out of power* this year," Betty Jonsson offered. "That says it, without making a point of his death."

We all agreed with Betty's compromise prediction, but I assured Olof that I would document the prophecy for my records just as he had originally made it.

"What other things do you see for 1970?" Marilyn asked again.

"Well, one thing that I have mentioned to Betty," Olof answered, "is a terrible fire here in Chicago. It will be a big one, and it will be at a hotel. At least two people will lose their lives."

Olof sipped at his coffee for a moment, then setting down his cup, he asked: "Brad, I don' 't suppose you want me to say that I see General de Gaulle dying this year."

"Say what you see, Olof," I clarified. "I only feel that a psychic should be careful in his phrasing of predictions."

"*Ja*, well, he will die before the year ends," Olof nodded. "I see this very clearly. But I don't know whether or not I will say it over the air."

"But you must tell Brad whenever you receive such an impression," Marilyn said. "No matter how good the hit, it just doesn't have the same value if you tell someone *after* the event has already taken place."

"I tell Betty many predictions long before the things happen," Olof said.

"Yes, Olof," Betty admitted, "but it just doesn't mean as much if you have only your wife to substantiate your predictions. To the skeptical, you could tell any lie you wished, and they would believe that I, as your wife, would swear to it. For instance, the first time that you and I heard about the Sharon Tate murders on television, you turned to me and said that the slaying had been done by a group of women who were directed in their actions by a man. That was a good hit, but you said it only to me."

"Betty is right," I spoke up. "From now on, you should drop your predictions in an envelope and mail them to me. That way you will always have that postmark to substantiate the fact that you made the prediction in advance of the occurrence."

That morning on the "psych-in" over WWCA, Olof phrased his prediction about Nasser in this manner: "Egypt's Nasser will be out of power in 1970." The psychic's view of the Egyptian president's death preceded fact by several months.

Olof did not give his prediction of de Gaulle's death over the air, but I did record the prognostication on that date, thereby making it another hit which preceded its realization by nearly a year.

He did release his prediction of ". . .a big fire in Chicago within a short time," and before January had ended, a tragic fire at the Chicago Hilton Hotel on Michigan Avenue took the lives of two teenaged deaf-mutes.

Olof also broadcast his preview of the up-and-down stock market, "great strides made in powering automobiles by electricity," and "a tragic turn in the marriage of Jackie and Ari Onassis." Although he did not state his complete impressions of this "tragic turn" over the air, Jonsson told this author that he foresees imminent "injury and possible death" to the Greek shipping magnate.

Lou Ursitti is impressed with Olof Jonsson's ability to predict the rise and fall of the stock market and the psychic's talent for previewing international events, but he feels ". . .that it all seems more significant when a prediction is made about a someone you personally know, such as the prediction Olof made about my sister, who was pregnant with her first child."

According to Ursitti: "Olof hadn't seen my sister in more than six months, but when I inquired when she would deliver, he said that she would give birth to a baby girl on July 14, 1970, between 11:00 P.M. and midnight. The doctor had said the baby would come due on July 9 and Grandma had predicted July 15.

"A baby girl, Nina Jean, took her first breath of life at exactly 8:16 P.M. on July 14. Olof was approximately three hours off on his prediction, but when you consider that he had not seen my sister for so long and was still to predict so accurately when she would give birth to a baby girl, I am willing to grant him three hours and score it a hit."

How does Olof manage to obtain his glimpses of the future?

"I either sit down in a chair or lie down on a couch and I concentrate on a particular person or situation and a particular time period—two months ahead, ten years, fifty years, it does not matter," Olof has said. "Then I meditate, that is rise to a transcendent level of consciousness in which time does not exist, and I move ahead in the temporal sequence until I arrive where I wish to be. Then I am able to move out of my body and, in my astral self, view the person or event or situation as it will be in the material future—as it is *now* to a transcendent level of my consciousness."

How is it possible to predict the future?

"I believe that everything is fixed for us—even to the smallest detail in life," Olof Jonsson states. "We know, for instance, that we can predict the date of a solar eclipse thousands of years from now. Thus it is for us. The forces have already been set in motion, even though we may not know all the factors involved. But even the changes are there. If, for example, I should foresee an accident for a friend and warn him so that he is able to avoid injury, he has not cheated the future. In that case the very act of my warning him was also already fixed. The past, present, and the future are all one."

Now without getting into a semantic slough with the ceaselessly debatable issues of fate and free will, permit me to attempt a clarification of what I believe Olof Jonsson means when he speaks of our lives, with even their changes, being "already fixed."

When we speak of true precognition, whether it comes about through a dream or the vision of a talented seer such as Olof Jonsson, we are given proof with the realization of the prediction becoming an event, an historical happening, that the seer did not see a *possibility*, but an actuality. In view of this fact, the question of whether or not the future can be changed has no meaning.

The foreknowledge of the future, of which some level of the unconscious is aware and of which it sometimes flashes a dramatic bit or scene to the conscious mind in a dream, trance, or vision, is founded on the knowledge of *how* the individual will use his freedom of choice. The "future event" conditions the unconscious self. The level of the unconscious that "knows" the future does *not* condition the "future event."

The transcendent element of the essential self which knows what "will be" blends all time into "what is now and what will always be." For the conscious self, what is now the past was once the future. We do not look upon past events and feel that we acted without freedom of will. Why then should we look at the future and feel that those events are predetermined? That an unconscious level of the psyche may *know* the future does not mean that the conscious self has no freedom of choice. Simply stated, if the future could be changed, it would not be the future. In a true precognitive experience when one perceives the future, he has seen what will be and what, for the transcendent element of the essential self, *already* exists.

Physical time—past, present, and future—exists only for the *conscious* mind. In those premonitions of the future which are beneficial (i.e. those that warn not to take a certain course of action or advise one to act when he might have ignored a situation), the transcendent self may overdramatize a future event in such a way that it seems to be a warning—which is, in turn, acted upon by the conscious self's characteristic reaction to crisis. The future is not altered in such cases, only implemented.

The following predictions are those future events and conditions which the transcendent level of Olof Jonsson's psyche has seen as already existing in the "Eternal Now." For those prognostications which seem to constitute warnings, those men and women concerned may be able to react to approaching crises by implementing their future plans.

Catastrophe in Southern Europe
"I see this happening in 1971, no later than the early part of 1972. It may happen in the south of Italy, maybe even farther south—Sicily, Greece. It will be a terrible tragedy and take many lives."

Arab States to Unite
"Within a very short time, the Arab nations will form a tight coalition. They will cease their bickering, soothe their jealousies, and terminate their inner conflicts in order to present a firm and united front."

Eruption of Hostilities in the Middle East
"Before 1972 there will be a deterioration in Arabic-Israeli relations which will lead to hostilities even more serious than the June War of 1967."

China to Enter Conflict in Southeast Asia
"Communist China will no longer be contented to serve as a supply base for North Vietnam and other Asian satellite nations. Red China's more active role in Southeast Asia, in either 1971 or early 1972, will cause violent repercussions in both the United States and the Soviet Union.

Time of Crisis between Russia and the United States

"It is my impression that 1972 will be a crisis year in relationships between Russia and the United States. An American statesman will distinguish himself in high-level talks and a few cracks in the Iron Curtain will result from his diplomatic proposals. If these brilliantly strategic moves are followed up at this time, the result of the crisis may be a period of harmony between the Soviet Union and the United States."

Berlin Riots in 1971

"A series of Communist-inspired riots will shatter the peace and economic stability of West Germany. Berlin will be the center of the most serious of these vicious riots."

Snowdens to Divorce in 1971

"Princess Margaret and Anthony Armstrong-Jones will terminate their marriage with a divorce in 1971."

Another "Cuban Crisis" in the Middle East

"By the end of 1971 or early in 1972, the United States will be faced with a situation similar to the Cuban Missile Crisis when Russia shall demand that the United States withdraw all support from Israel or risk a full-scale encounter with the Soviet Union"

Democrat in the White House in 1972

"Nixon may not receive the nomination from his own party, but even if he should be chosen to run, he will be defeated. I seem to view Senator Edward Muskie as the next President of the United States."

Scandal in High United States Government Echelons

"Very soon, most likely early in 1971, a big scandal will break, and some very high-ranking government officials will be exposed for their mismanagement and personal appropriation of government funds. I receive the strongest feeling that the greatest abuses will be in the area of monies designated for defense."

Secret Soviet Weapon

"I have been receiving psychic impressions of a secret Soviet weapon which would employ powerful energy rays in a mechanism similar to the laser."

Russian Mind Control Drug

"I have had a recurrent vision of Russian agents disseminating a drug, designed for proliferation in our food supplies, which would numb or destroy our capacity to reason. The drug would not harm us physically, but it would deteriorate our memories and our ability to reason properly. In short, it would make us completely malleable to any kind of propaganda.

Iron Curtain Propaganda via Telepathy

"Because of my own psychism, I know that the Russians have been experimenting with psychics behind the Iron Curtain who have been concentrating on beaming Communist propaganda to us via telepathy. They have many good senders behind the Iron Curtain who have been attempting to place certain thoughts into the minds of our national leaders. The Communists know that the best way to make the United States fall is from the inside. Remember, Khrushchev said once that Russia would never have to fight the United States, that the U.S. would fall of its own weaknesses. This is one way the Communists are seeking to accomplish the internal collapse of the United States. They have developed an extensive system of telepathic individuals who spend nearly all of their waking moments directing propaganda at our national leaders. I know such things are possible, because I myself have done them. If I concentrate long enough, I can make anyone reverse his normal thought patterns. Remember the political speaker I made orate against himself when I was in Australia? I have sent my own thoughts to Russia, and these are the impressions I have received."

Miracle Chemical for Mental Illness

"By 1975 there will be a compound in general use which will treat mental illness by restoring chemical balance to the brain. The chemical will be successful in treating cases of paranoia, schizophrenia, and manic depression. It will also be helpful in elevating the intelligence of the mentally retarded and in eliminating criminal tendencies in those who were born with the flaw of extreme antisocial behavior."

Moon Base to Be a Launching Platform, Not a Colony

"Man will never abandon Earth to settle on the Moon. The

successful Moon landing will lead to our building stations and bases on the Moon in order to carry on scientific and military control over the Earth, but there will be no mass exodus to our satellite. Rather, the Moon will be utilized as a platform for more distant journeys out into space."

Evidence of Previous Life on the Moon

"Our Moon stations will discover evidence that *Homo sapiens* has not been the first to utilize our satellite as a base. Super-intelligent creatures from another galaxy have employed the Moon in aeons past in much the same manner that we will use the satellite in aeons to come."

Advice to Youthful Revolutionists

"The young people are very intelligent and they can see many things that are faulty in the political system of the United States. But before they can accomplish positive changes, they must learn to master themselves. Because so many of them have so much hatred in their minds, they have cast an almost trance-like state over themselves. Once hatred gains complete control, it will release itself in violence and bombs. I would advise the youth to gather together with like-minded individuals and practice discipline and self-control. Once these things have been mastered, they will find that they can accomplish much good through meditation and by placing positive thoughts in their elders' and their leaders' minds through telepathy."

Continued Interest in the Occult and the Paranormal

"The interest in the Occult, especially among youth, will grow greater and greater as more people learn that there is more to our universe than those things which we can touch with our physical senses."

Major Climate Changes by the Year Two Thousand

"By the year two thousand, a number of natural catastrophes will have set in motion certain irreversible Earth changes which will lead to a dramatic alteration of climate in several areas of the world."

Electric Cars Perfected, but Soon No Private Autos in the Cities

"Within the next few years, engineers will have perfected an efficient and economical electrically powered automobile. The internal combustion motor will be outlawed in all major cities by 1980. Within another decade or less, legislation will eliminate the private automobile in all major cities, and only medical and law enforcement personnel will use compact, electrically powered cars. By the year two thousand, the automobile, as we know it, will have virtually disappeared from use."

Pollution of Our Environment

"I have been speaking out against the abuses of our natural resources for over twenty years. Only recently has it become fashionable to be concerned about such matters. It is my psychic vision that it is not yet too late to save our planet if serious efforts are maintained, but the redemption of our air and water cannot be a faddish interest. Desperate and concerted efforts are required at once.

"But even more dangerous, I believe, is *thought* pollution. We must begin at once to train people to think spiritualistically, rather than materialistically."

On Combatting Soul Pollution

"If you have a choice, help others before you help yourself.

"Never consciously perform any act that will bring harm to others or to yourself.

"Feel harmonious in all that you do in life."

New Step in the Evolution of Man

"Man, with the aid of certain chemicals or spiritual exercises, will be able to live off cosmic energy. Perhaps by the year two thousand, we will not have to eat plants and meat to derive our fuel and energy. We will be able to obtain energy directly from the sun."

Chapter Twenty-Three

UFOS, MAN'S GENESIS, AND OUR
COMING HELP FROM OTHER WORLDS

On that warm night in August, 1970, the sky looked very much like a gigantic blackboard on which some superior intelligence had industriously laid out a mammoth connect-the-dots mystery in luminous chalk. Olof Jonsson, Betty, my wife Marilyn, and I sat on the balcony of a Wisconsin lodge. The kids were asleep, exhausted from a full day of traveling, sunning, and swimming. Betty and Marilyn were browned from an afternoon of sunbathing, and Olof and I were satisfied at the way several hours of interviewing had developed. It felt good to relax.

Betty was just refilling the glasses with chilled, sparkling Cold Duck when Marilyn noticed a bright object traversing the night sky. "Is that a satellite?" she asked, "Or is it an airplane? Or. . ."

The object suddenly stopped dead still, answering the two questions she had had time to pose. Neither a satellite nor an airplane can instantly suspend motion in mid-flight.

Marilyn completed her third question: ". . .or is it a UFO?" By now, the object appeared to be flashing different colored lights in a sequence of red, greenish-blue, and white, as if it were attempting to establish contact with intelligent life on Earth's surface.

"I will try to answer them with telepathy," Olof said.

"Just don't ask them to land!" Marilyn requested.

"No," Betty said, echoing Marilyn's sentiments. "No trips to outer space for me right now. I have to be back at work tomorrow."

After a few moments, the object made a rapid movement to the left, then began moving a course drastically altered from the one which it had been traveling. Whatever we were watching steadily accelerated until it was out of sight in a matter of seconds.

"Friends of yours, Olof?" I asked facetiously.

Olof smiled, but his manner was strangely serious. "Perhaps they were very old friends."

When Olof was a child of four or five, he used to take great delight in playing by himself near a small stream that ran by his home. As he made leaf-houses among the water grasses and sailed toy boats between the lily pads, the child was aware of other presences near him.

"They may have been the same entities that so often represent themselves to small children as fairies and wood sprites," Olof told me. "But, somehow, on occasion, I believe that I was able to see them as they really were. They were taller than I, but not nearly as tall as my parents. They were, perhaps, just under—or just over—five feet tall. They had much larger heads and proportionately much smaller bodies than an adult human. Their skin color varied from bluish-green to golden brown to a shade of gray. It was they who began to tell me wonderful things about the universe and Cosmic harmony."

Who were these strange beings?

"I felt that they were friends, that they wanted to teach me and to help me," Olof answered simply. "Now, I feel that they may have been from another solar system or another dimension. Of course I am still convinced that they are friendly and intend to help man as much as they can without interfering in his own development and free will."

Because of his early contact with beings whom he believes to have come from some other world or dimension, Olof Jonsson does not scoff at reports of unidentified flying objects.

"In their traveling to other worlds or dimensions, the flying saucer occupants have learned to eliminate Time, Olof said. "Once a technology has learned to conquer and control Time, everything can happen *Now.*"

It is Jonsson's psychic impression that human life did not originate on the planet Earth.

"I believe that man was placed here by some higher intelligence," he has remarked. "In the beginning there were maybe fifty or one hundred men and women. *Homo sapiens* is a vast experiment being conducted by Cosmic beings. Earth is a gigantic laboratory."

Who are these Cosmic experimenters?

"They have life-spans equal to thousands of our years," Jonsson believes. "In their world, they have solved all the myriad problems of existence that we are still fighting on Earth. They have cured all known diseases. It is impossible to achieve one hundred percent harmony on the material plane until all diseases have been conquered.

"I have already described the appearance of those beings whom I saw as a small boy," Olof said. "In essence, they are similar in appearance to man, but they have achieved complete control of mind and they may shape their fleshly bodies in a manner that is most appealing to those with whom they communicate. Throughout man's history, these entities may have appeared as angels, god-like beings, fairies—even demons and devils if it suited their particular purpose."

Olof Jonsson believes that the UFO phenomenon is simply physical evidence that the Cosmic scientists are returning in larger numbers to study the progress of their great experiment.

"Although there have always been a number of Watchers on duty," he states, "more of them are now arriving to keep man under careful surveillance as he enters the New Age of Aquarius. A period of cleansing may be necessary here on Earth, because there are too few *Homo sapiens* with enough responsibility to balance those with too much power.

"Our Cosmic Masters may see that the time is soon upon Earth when another cycle of the rise and fall of a civilization and a culture must be completed, and they stand ready to assist man in the transition from the degenerative, destructive pattern in which he was traveling with his misapplied science to a plane of higher consciousness in which the false and outworn will be destroyed and discarded.

"Man will still be man and will still function as a human being," Olof assured his listeners, "but his frequency, his vibratory rate, will be raised to a finer, more etherialized level. Man's sense perceptions will be heightened. His sense of Cosmic Harmony will be filled with true understanding of peace, love, and brotherhood. The increase in the vibratory rate of this planet will permit man to transcend the old physical boundaries and to become a citizen of a higher dimension, with a new depth of insight that will enable him to live in brotherhood with his fellow man and with beings from other solar systems and other planes of existence."

Is there any way in which man might prepare himself for the new age?

"Yes," Olof nodded, "there is one excellent way by which each man might attune the frequency of his own individual being. Each night before meditation, call upon Supreme Intelligence by whatever name you know God, and ask for his Harmony to aid you in attuning with the increased vibratory rate that has begun to permeate all living beings who stand at the dawning of the Age of Aquarius. Then meditate, allowing your consciousness to attune itself to peace and harmony. The New Age will require many of advanced attunement to offer assistance to those of denser frequency, who will flounder helplessly at the time of the great transition and change."

Once, as we sat in a moment of quiet reflection in the living room of the psychic's home in Riverdale, Illinois, I asked Olof if he ever felt that he himself might have been "planted" on this world by beings from another planet or dimension.

After a moment's consideration, Olof answered, "No, I have never thought that the *physical* Olof Jonsson may have been placed here by entities from a flying saucer. But I must admit that I have never really felt that I was of this world. I believe that I may have lived before elsewhere in the universe and that I have reincarnated on Earth for this temporal existence."

"Have you ever felt, though, as if you might be receiving instructions from beings or entities from other spheres of existence?"

"Sometimes," he admitted. "There are times that I feel that there are things that I must do in this world. Many times when I am doing an experiment, I can feel that there is someone outside of myself who wants me to do it, to show this materialistic world that there is a more lasting element to its existence. I suppose I must confess that since earliest childhood I have felt that I must live my life to fulfill a role here on Earth. It has always seemed my specific duty to spend my most vital energies in an attempt to convince my fellow humans of the reality of the spiritual spheres of being."

Chapter Twenty-Four

DEVELOPING YOUR
"UNKNOWN" SENSORY PERCEPTION

One night in August, 1970, as I sat visiting with Olof and Betty Jonsson, I kept at the psychic to try as best he could to articulate precisely what happened inside his psyche when he exercised his "psi" abilities.

"I cannot say exactly," Olof would answer. "It is very difficult to describe in words."

"Please try," I encouraged him. "I think the majority of men and women who are attracted to the field of psychic phenomena are really very literate and well read. I don't believe they need any longer to be convinced of the *reality* of paranormal experiences through the reporting of remarkable occurrences of lost children found, murders solved, the future foreseen, or the past reactivated. I feel quite certain that the bit of pragmatist in everyone, including those mystically oriented, has by now begun to ask just what exactly is in 'psi' for them. How might they develop ESP and use it effectively to make their own lives more harmonious? How might they themselves duplicate some of the incredible feats of the great psychics and seers?"

Olof smiled the smile of a man who has found the answer to a dilemma. "Since you are the writer, you will have to experience a state of heightened psychic sensitivity so that you may tell others what it is like.

"But that could take years," I began to protest.

"It could take years to control psychic abilities effectively," Olof agreed, "but I can give you a sample of such talents tonight."

I looked over at Betty, who seemed to be taking all this very seriously, then back at Olof.

"Are you willing to learn?" the psychic challenged me. "Are you willing to drop a bit of your reporter's professional detachment and become an attentive student?"

"All right," I said, snapping on my tape recorder to serve as witness to whatever might transpire. "Let's have a go at it."

Olof began by explaining his opinion that the processes involved in ESP reside, as do the processes of creativity, in the unconscious mind.

"We must learn how to use that unconscious," he said. "You may begin by practicing different methods. For instance, you can try to guess people's birthdays or what they have been doing during the day. You can throw dice and try to guess what numbers will come up. You can deal cards at random from a deck, toss them face down, and attempt to guess their value. There are all kinds of exercises for your mind that will help you to develop extrasensory perception, or what I prefer to call *Unknown sensory perception*, because I don't believe it is 'extra' at all—only unknown at the present time."

With that bit of introduction, Olof asked me to shuffle a deck of ESP cards and hold them behind my back.

"Now see if you can develop the right conditions," he told me. "Erase everything from your mind. Forget all about those petty things that are troubling you and relax your mind. Attain peace and calm. Achieve harmony. Do not think. When I lift my hand, you call the name of a card and take it out of the pack at the same time. . . . Now!"

I called a circle, but drew a square.

"*Don't think*," Olof admonished me. "Try it again when I raise my hand."

"The moment you say, 'don't think,' that's the time my brain floods itself with images," I complained. "How do you *stop* thinking?"

"You must release the irritations in your mind and banish all things that disturb you," Olof said patiently. "You must tell youself to become calm and peaceful. You must command yourself to react to no outside distractions. Once you have achieved the proper conditions, you will feel psychic energy and *knowing* building up within you.

"Shuffle the cards," he bade me. "Try it again. . .Now!"

I called a cross and drew a cross.

"This may sound presumptuous so early in the game," I apologized, "but I don't think it was chance. I felt I *knew* that the card really would be a cross."

"You have to catch it in that little blank place," Betty offered. "When you achieve that calm and peace—those right conditions Olof always talks about—it seems to me as though your conscious mind just blanks out. One night I got twelve cards in a row. Olof had evidently managed to help me create the proper conditions. But as soon as I began to *think*, 'Well, look what I'm doing,' then I couldn't do it anymore."

"That is the difference between the way your conscious and your unconscious mind works," Olof told us. "You must remain absolutely calm at the time your unconscious is controlling your actions.

"For instance, Brad, you take part of the deck; Betty, you take the other half. Now, when I lift my hand, you each throw a star from your share of the deck onto the table. Remember, remain calm, almost indifferent, as if you didn't care if you succeeded or not."

Betty and I did as Olof suggested for two tries, failing to withdraw stars on either attempt.

"Don't worry," Olof pacified us. "This is practice. This is very important. You are building the proper conditions in your mind. Try it again. . . . Now!"

This time Olof's raised hand was the signal for success. Betty and I each withdrew a star from the deck.

"Very good," the psychic congratulated us. "Now I will do it."

He took the two halves of the pack from us, and began to shuffle them. "Meditate on the star again. When you tell me to stop, I will withdraw a star."

I watched Olof shuffling the pack, carefully holding the cards face down, not even glancing at the deck in his hands. By now I had achieved a mental device for non-thought: I concentrated on an enormous snowbank, an endless expanse of white. After I had retained this image for a few moments, there came a certain "knowing" that told me. . . .

"Now!" I all but shouted at Olof's shuffling fingers.

Olof smiled, held up a star.

Then it was my turn again. Olof handed me the deck, asked me to shuffle the cards until I felt I had a circle, then remove it. After a few moments of quiet shuffling, I withdrew a circle.

"I'm finding it easier to blank out my conscious mind," I said.

"That is very important," Olof nodded.

"I blank out, then I keep shuffling and shuffling, and then my hand just seems to move of its own volition and picks out the card I want."

"Yes," Olof agreed, "that is the way to do it. Do not become distracted. Just ignore everything around you. Isn't it a wonderful feeling when the *knowing* comes?"

"Yes," I admitted. "As you say, it is a strange kind of knowing, yet it is most definitely not a *thinking*."

"It seems to me that I get a picture of the card first," Betty said. "Then I forget it and go on shuffling. The feeling of knowing begins to come, then I just don't think about it, and suddenly I have the card in my hand."

"That seems to be it," I agreed. "You get an image, say, for example, of the circle, and you go shuffle. . .shuffle. . . shuffle. . .and then, pop! There it is."

For our next experiment, Olof proposed that we pass the deck back and forth, each drawing one card, the star, until we had drawn all five stars from the deck. Perhaps it will seem incredible to report, but we accomplished this in only five drawings.

Olof began, shuffled the deck, withdrew a star. He passed the pack to Betty, who shuffled, withdrew a star. She passed the deck to me, and I shuffled, withdrew a star. Two more withdrawals, and all five stars had been removed from the deck. The conditions were right.

The conditions *had* to be right for the next experiment!

Olof asked me to draw five cards at random from the deck of ESP cards after we had each shuffled them thoroughly, mine being the last shuffle. When I had blindly selected my five cards, Olof quickly withdrew five of his own. Then, with the cards held behind our backs, we withdrew one card at a time and matched four out of five.

I cannot even imagine the odds against such a rumpling of the laws of chance. First, two men must select two sets of four out of five cards that match in a random selection, then, without knowledge of the identities of those cards, bring them out from behind their backs in matching sequence, four out of five times.

Olof Jonsson had been absolutely correct: It had been necessary for me to experience a heightened state of psychic sensitivity so that I might fully appreciate the Harmony, the feeling of Oneness with the Universe of which he speaks so often. And it is to be hoped, that such an experience has enabled me to write this book with much greater insight than would have been possible without at least a fleeting knowledge of the psychic mechanism that elevates one to a transcendent level of consciousness.

Questions and Answers on Psychic Development:

"Would you recommend that a young person trying to develop his psychic abilities use an Ouija board?"

There are many ways of encouraging psychic development, and if a young person benefits from the visual aid and the physical property of an Ouija board, it may be helpful. An Ouija board may, however, open the unconscious to other influences, such as possessive entities, which can be harmful.

I would rather recommend the simple device of filling a glass of water and placing it on the table before you. Stare at the water for five minutes or so and erase all thoughts from your mind. Do not think of a thing. Just look at the water. Once you feel that you have achieved the proper condition, practice guessing cards from an ESP deck. The glass of water is simply a physical object on which to focus your attention and to permit the unconscious to rise above your conscious mind. Once you have learned to blank out your conscious mind by concentrat-

ing on the glass of water, you will find it easier and easier to achieve the altered state of consciousness necessary for the exercise of your psychic abilities.

"What is your opinion of astrology?"

I personally do not use it, nor do I work with horoscopes, but I do feel that there may be something to astrology.

I discovered a very interesting point some years ago in Sweden: It is easier to send and receive telepathic impressions with someone who is born close to your own birth date. I conducted an experiment with one hundred persons who were born in October, my own birth month, and I found that the scores were twenty percent higher than in the same telepathic experiment carried on with people from other birth months. I found the same thing to be true in an experiment in clairvoyance. However, when it comes to levitation, a mixture of birth months seems to work better.

"What do you think of the claims of those who call themselves spiritual masters?"

It is a basic occult law that Masters rarely reveal themselves or permit their true identities to be revealed by others. If one considers this law as valid, then it would seem to hold that one who claims to be a Master very seldom is.

A high-level development of psychic abilities should not persuade one to believe that he is a Master. The sensitive of high development must guard against his ego gaining the upper hand and tainting his psyche with pride and arrogance. A true Master walks the Earth serving in love and wisdom, ever mindful of the danger of magnifying his own ego or confusing an already confused and searching mankind.

"Has your psychism ever made you feel odd or weird?"

No, what I am is normal for me and I have been happy with my life. Maybe the less sensitive people are the abnormal ones, and I am normal.

"What, in your opinion, is the most important benefit that one can derive from a heightened psychic sensitivity?"

A great calm and peace that suffuses one's soul and makes him harmonious with the Universe. This sense of harmony places the minor distractions of our earthly life in their proper perspective and enables the sensitive to be serene and tranquil wherever he may be.

Chapter Twenty-Five

ACHIEVING COSMIC HARMONY WITH THE UNIVERSE

"Olof, it seems to me that you envision a purposeful universe, a Divine Plan."

Yes, a Divine Plan that in the end will be harmonious.

"Harmony seems to be your favorite concept."

Yes, harmony is God. When you are in harmony with the Cosmos, you feel completely satisfied.

"It is a God-like feeling, then?"

Yes. You feel completely happy, no matter what your lot in life may be in the eyes of a materialistic society.

"Are there beings, entities, masters on other planes of existence that may guide us in achieving Cosmic Harmony?"

There are forces in the universe, minds that can help us gain information about the true meaning of life. I believe that there is a dynamic force and that intelligences are associated with it.

"Who are these intelligences?"

They could be entities from other places in the universe. Perhaps they are the souls of those who have died on highly

*evolved planets, who have left their radiation in the universe
and their intelligence remains as a force for good and for
spiritual evolution.*

*You may interpret these intelligences in any way that is most
compatible with your own psyche—as an Indian, as a wise old
man, as a holy figure—but they are bodiless forms of benign
intelligence. These intelligences may cloak themselves as Tibet-
ans and astral teachers because the human brain will more
readily accept an entity that looks like a human being, rather
than a shapeless, shimmering intelligence.*

"You do believe firmly, then, that there are beings somewhere in the Cosmos who are interested in guiding us and
helping us achieve harmony and unity?"

*Yes, and I believe these beings have the ability to absorb our
actions and our thoughts so that they may know better how to
direct us toward Cosmic Harmony. These beings avoid language
and work with us on an unconscious level. The phenomenon of
telepathy affords us with proof that language means nothing to
the unconscious. We do not think in words, but in ideas and
feelings. What language does God speak? The feelings and the
harmony communicated between the unconscious levels of self
comprise the one "language" that all men understand. That is
God's language.*

Olof Jonsson speaks of the "Goal and Meaning of Life":
*After a number of years of probing the Unknown, one learns
not to be astounded at anything which he might encounter.
And the more one probes the problems which lie beyond the
boundaries of everyday life, the more convinced he becomes
that it is necessary for every single person to find his own
solution to the goal and meaning of life. A solution which seems
perfectly clear to one individual may be completely unworkable
for another.*

*It is regrettable that the structure of modern society leaves
precious little freedom for individual thought. The societal ideal
wishes to group all citizens into various categories and to stamp
them with one and the same inoffensive mold. Private beliefs
become superfluous in such a social structure. Independent*

thought is no longer welcomed or encouraged. The private will is choked.

When a person has nothing to believe in beyond himself and exists only for material acquisitions, things are not as they should be. When personal selfishness has become a religion, spiritual danger is unavoidable. Personal selfishness spawns violence between individuals and war between nations.

Today's restlessness and disturbances have turned into whips that goad us on in the race with speed itself. All the techniques of our modern technology seem to push on faster and faster, perhaps only toward a vacuum which lies in readiness for us in the stockpiles of nuclear armaments.

Civilized man is in the process of losing his soul. A spiritual undermining has long been at work, so that it is no longer in vogue to believe in something. Throughout the ages, the faith that sustained man sprung not out of materialism and easy living, but out of hardship and pain. The person who is forced to fight his way through suffering somehow becomes supplied with strength. In the last days of the Roman Empire when Christianity was forced to fight for its very life, it was filled with power and spirit. Now the old verities seem to have been shelved and exchanged for well-worded but empty sermons designed to sound palatable for broadcast purposes.

The orthodox, organized churches have taken little responsibility toward investigating the Unknown levels of spirituality and achieving Cosmic Harmony with the Universe. They have become entirely too worldly and more concerned with the careful administration of their property holdings and their business affairs than the ministry of basic spiritual principles.

It is not the big, well-organized mass meetings that will give modern man the directions to the paths of life and death. Here and there in our nation and elsewhere in the world, there are groups of people in small, obscure movements, who are seeking to find the meaning of existence and the secret of immortality.

The power of mind that lies within each man is capable of working miracles when it takes a good and right course, but it can also be destructive when it is ruled by the power of evil sustained by a spirit of personal selfishness and an obsession with materialism. Perhaps the true purpose of the spiritual life is to offer help and comfort to the suffering, concern for the weak, and good will and unselfish acts to everyone.

No man needs to be afraid of dying. The order of Nature, the Cosmic Harmony of the Universe tells us that in all forms of existence, everything has meaning, nothing comes about by chance. It is blasphemous to believe that man alone should be excluded from the orderliness and purposefulness of the Universe. The secret of life's course and death's chambers is found within each of us in the unknown levels of the unconscious, wherein lie many dormant powers.

The utilization of the powers, the "sparks of divinity," within each of us, should never tempt the wise to make a religion out of spiritual blessings that have been dispensed to all men. Rather, an awareness of the powers within should serve to equip the interested and the receptive with a brilliant search-light on the path to Cosmic Harmony.

It is in one's own home, in his own little chamber, in moments of quiet meditation that a stream of the great light of Cosmos is best able to reach in and enrich the soul and open the eyes to the magnificent and tranquil gardens that lie beyond the borders of the Unknown. That which governs a man's life is neither chemistry nor physics nor anything material, but the proper spiritual link up with the powers within his own psyche and the blessed Harmony that governs the Universe.

INDEX